Intent

Selected Sermons by
Rabbi Elliot J. Cosgrove

Hineni

Selected Sermons by
Rabbi Elliot J. Cosgrove

2011–2012 / 5772

Hineni: Selected Sermons by Rabbi Elliot J. Cosgrove
2011–2012 / 5772

ParkAvenue
Synagogue ק"ק אגודת ישרים

Copyright © 2012 Park Avenue Synagogue

ISBN 978–0–9825084–3–5

Printed in the United States of America in 2012

Park Avenue Synagogue
50 East 87th Street
New York, NY 10128
www.pasyn.org

Contents

Foreword

This fourth volume of sermons by my rabbi, comrade, and dear friend Rabbi Elliot Cosgrove has the title *Hineni*, "Here I am," to reflect the message of the fourth *parashah* of the Torah, *Va-yera*, where Abraham answers God's question and test. While the challenges facing Conservative Judaism, Jewish identity in the Diaspora in the twenty-first century, or support of a secure, democratic, Jewish, independent State of Israel, may not be of the same nature as Abraham's decision to sacrifice his son, Rabbi Cosgrove does address from his pulpit the manifold ways that Jewish identity and observance are tested in our time.

In sweeping words he seeks to lead his listeners to an authentic Judaism. "If the Judaism I teach and preach is a Judaism that seeks authenticity without judgment, inclusiveness not guilt, and personal meaning before ideological loyalty, then maybe it is because I think the landscape of Jewish life has changed and past formulations do not stand a chance in the present marketplace of ideas." However, authenticity is necessary but not sufficient. Rabbi Cosgrove firmly grasps that the Judaism of Park Avenue Synagogue must also bridge the past and the future. "His Judaism" must speak to all members of our community but most importantly, to our children, so they will embrace it. "I must help shape that future, but ultimately it is not my future – it is theirs. I bless them, smiling inwardly, imagining that day in the not-too-distant future when they too, please God, will hold their breath, blessing their children ... with the words of our tradition handed down for millennia."

To what ends or purposes do we live an engaged Jewish life? The rabbi answers that we serve not only the Jewish future, but all of humanity at one and the same time. He demonstrates this commitment not only in words but in deeds of social justice and interfaith outreach in the local community, at the Vatican, and with missions to the Middle East, Russia, and Cuba.

Support for Israel has been a major focus for our synagogue since Rabbi Cosgrove's arrival. In the year now ending, members and staff made three trips there and we also hosted an extraordinary roster of distinguished speakers on Israel. The rabbi addressed this community's covenantal relationship to Israel in many sermons. The words I remember best were before Rosh Hashanah when he said, "But I do know this. That one day, 10, 20, 30 years from now, we will look back on this moment – just as we look back on '48, '67, '73 – and we will know that we lived through an era when history turned on a pivot. Our children and grandchildren will read about it in a history book and they will walk into our rooms and say, "Dad, Mom – what did you do for Israel then?"

In the midst of leading the revitalization of this community of nearly 130 years, my rabbi retains his modesty, humility, and sense of humor. In recalling the manner of Yankee legend Mickey Mantle rounding the bases after a home run with shoulders limp and his head down, he noted that the "Mick," "at the moment of achievement, at the moment of triumph, he comported himself, well, like a *mensch*."

As Rabbi Cosgrove grows to lead Conservative Judaism, as I believe he undoubtedly will, I am certain that he will live his life as he speaks from his pulpit. "Our deeds in the years ahead will tell the story. The best we can do, the only thing we can do, is to seek to lead lives of modest and humble compassion, to keep our heads down as we round 'em, acting with love and kindness to those who matter most and who are most dependent on our care, so that we, in the generations to come, will, like those we remember today, be remembered for a blessing."

I stand with Rabbi Cosgrove to lead this community infused with the ideals expressed on these pages. I thank him each day for the lives he has touched, comforted, and inspired. And as I have told him, among God's gifts to me is having the chance to work with him in doing our part to write the everlasting narrative of our people.

B'shalom,
Steven M. Friedman, *Chairman*

Acknowledgments

This book would not be possible without the tireless and thoughtful efforts of Jean Bloch Rosensaft and Marga Hirsch. Their dedication to the Park Avenue Synagogue community is much appreciated.

Preface

In a world driven by social media, there is something positively old-fashioned about the genre of a sermon. For thousands of years, preachers of the Jewish world have communicated their highest hopes and deepest concerns by way of homilies – publicly delivered addresses tied into the texts of our tradition and the hearts and minds of the listener. But in this day and age, when our information comes in an instant and is most often received by way of a hand-held device, are we really to believe that this hoary mode of communication has a future?

It is a fair question, one that I think about frequently as I write sermons week-in and week-out. I certainly believe that given the ever-changing landscape of modern communication, it is incumbent on all forward thinking communities to be fully aware of how contemporary Jews seek intellectual and spiritual sustenance. As I have learned to track web readership, I have spent much time pondering what it means when more people "hear" a sermon on the PAS website than in the sanctuary on a Shabbat morning. The irony of this sermon book (and the others) is not lost on me, in that they seek to canonize that which is best experienced "live." The fact that this year's sermon book will be made available on Kindle signals a knowing response to our responsibility to meet our Jews "where they are."

Nevertheless, I do believe there is a compelling dimension to the spoken word that remains unchallenged. The magic of a sermon is that it emerges from a constellation of variables that, when functioning together, accomplish that which can not be done electronically. A speaker shares an idea that is heard at one and the same time by a roomful of listeners. Emails, blogs, and twitter feeds are accessed privately at different times and different places. Like a lesson taught in a classroom, or a sporting event played in an arena, sermons are predicated on the belief that community is formed by way of shared experiences. While it is frontal in nature, a good sermon is never meant to be a passive experience. Rather it should engender discussion, daydreaming, and hopefully, action. Often the most important outcome of a sermon is the dialogue that emerges (in the pews or at *kiddush*) on the merits or shortcomings of the ideas expressed.

To some degree, the challenges and opportunities of the spoken word are emblematic of much deeper cultural challenges facing the Jewish world. There is a countercultural nature to Jewish life and living in that the power of Jewish prayer, education, and philanthropy has always hinged on Jewish life being a collective and shared enterprise. In our world, driven by the individualized choices of the "sovereign self," maintaining this historic strength becomes a mounting challenge with every passing day. Our charge, therefore, is to position our communally-minded nature as a critical and much needed corrective to the lonely options offered by secular modernity. Park Avenue Synagogue stands proud as a house of shared learning, prayer, and comfort in a world sorely lacking in these very qualities.

My deepest thanks go to Jean Bloch Rosensaft for directing the publication of the sermon collections. I am grateful for your kindness, editorial eye, aesthetic sensibility, and love for our synagogue and the Jewish world. So too, I want to thank my colleague Marga Hirsch for your meticulous and rapid efforts to bring the sermons onto the web week after week, sensitively transforming the run-on sentences spoken on the pulpit into a polished and defensible collection of publishable writing.

This book of sermons will be distributed on the final Kol Nidre of Steven M. Friedman's tenure as Chairman of Park Avenue Synagogue. Steve, your leadership and service to our community have empowered us to see new horizons of possibility. The care and attention you and your team of officers devote to every matter of synagogue life set the tone for the professional staff and the rest of the community. We are all grateful beyond words. For five years you and I will have sat with each other on the *bimah* nearly every Shabbat, not to mention our rich conversations on the future – which are too numerous to count. I am grateful for many things: for your love of the Jewish community, for the bullets you have taken on my behalf, for our friendship that will last into the decades ahead, and for the ever-flowing well that is your volunteer spirit. High on my list is my personal debt to Cheri, who makes it all possible for you. But most of all, I am grateful for your personal integrity, your insistence on excellence, your belief that ideas matter, and your steadfast conviction that however good we may be, we can be better tomorrow.

Steve, on your final year as Chairman, I dedicate this book to you and Cheri.

Elliot J. Cosgrove
June 18, 2012
28 *Sivan* 5771

"9/11: Empathy and Indifference"

9/11 has bequeathed to us a huge range of responses, as numerous and varied as we, the diverse humanity living in the wake of the tragedy. For many, perhaps many in this room, the loss, the grief, the mourning continues. This week, I spoke to one member of our community who lost her husband in the towers. Words still fail her, tears still flow easily. To the casual observer her life has in some respects been rebuilt, but scratch the surface and her loss remains ever-present – never overcome, just managed day by day. I spoke to another congregant, who by a stroke of luck was not in the towers that morning, but lost his entire professional community. This week he shared with me that he chooses not to think of the searing flesh, his colleagues who jumped to their death. Rather he focuses on the heroism of that day, the firefighters and police officers who rushed into the buildings as everyone else rushed out, he thinks of the person who carried a wheelchair-bound colleague down flights and flights of stairs to safety. Some bear anger, others face ongoing anxiety. Those of us with young children struggle with the question of when will we explain it all to them – at what point do we allow their innocence to be shattered? Some look for the silver lining – asking how that day made us stronger. Others reject the very suggestion that loss could matter – objecting to the possibility that such maniacal evil could ever be associated with a positive dividend. Some insist that the events of 9/11 are a wake-up call to turn inward, throw up fences, and defend borders. Others just the opposite – that we must be more open, more sensitive to the stranger within and beyond our borders. So many responses, as numerous and varied as we, the diverse humanity living in the wake of the evil perpetrated that day.

If I had to condense the Jewish response to evil wrought by one human being upon another, I would do it in two words: empathy and indifference. These are the two sides of the coin around which moral behavior pivots. These are the elements by which we can discuss and respond to that day.

Let me explain.

In a recent book, Cambridge psychologist Simon Baron-Cohen defined empathy as the "ability to identify what someone else is thinking or feeling and to respond to their thoughts and feeling with an appropriate emotion." In other words, if you are able to extend concern beyond your immediate circle of self-interest, if you are able to consider someone else's needs, wants, and wishes that may be different from yours and behave accordingly – then you are empathetic. If you are indifferent to the concerns of others, if are unable to allow for the possibility that the needs, thoughts, feelings – the humanity – of another can impact your own behavior, well, that is the beginning of evil. And when you arrive at that point, where you are so absorbed in your own beliefs, so indifferent to the humanity of another, "zeroing out" in the bell curve of empathy – well, that is where evil is to be found. As the British philosopher Edmund Burke once explained, "All that is necessary for the triumph of evil is for good men to do nothing." It is a rather simple calculus, but it is a remarkably accurate litmus test by which to track evil over the course of human history.

Since ancient times, Jews have well understood the empathy-indifference continuum. According to Talmud, the destruction of the Temple in Jerusalem came about because of *sinat ḥinam*, causeless hatred (Yoma 9b). It was the rancor wrought by indifference, by the inability of one person to identify with the needs of another, that so frayed the social fabric of society, that it was eventually torn asunder. Destruction, pogroms, cruelties on a large and small scale across history – in each and each and every case, it is the absence of empathy that is the marker by which we find the darkest moments of humanity. There is, of course, the question of scope. But by one understanding, the evil acts of 9/11 are yet another example in the tragic arc of human history when terrorists were so blinded by their radicalism that they spilled the blood of innocent lives.

Which leads us ultimately to the question of response. There are no words that can mitigate, diminish, or minimize the horror of 9/11 – no pithy explanations that can soothe a broken soul. And yet, whether it is in response to the Temple or the Twin Towers, we are not frozen into inaction. Because in realizing that evil is found in the lack of empathy, we also identify the antidote – namely, an insistence on expressing concern for others, an intolerance to indifference. Rabbi Abraham Isaac Kook, the Chief Rabbi of Palestine under the British mandate, explained that if the Temple was destroyed due to *sinat ḥinam*, causeless hatred, then redemption will only come with *ahavat ḥinam*, causeless love. Only when we come to love our neighbor without reservation, then and only then will there be redemption for Israel and all of mankind.

Jewish history is replete with individuals who chose to respond to evil by asserting empathy. Think of Abraham Joshua Heschel, who narrowly escaped the Shoah and lost nearly his entire family. His response, significantly, was not to freeze up, not to turn solely to parochial concerns, but just the opposite. It was his awareness of humanity's indifference to the plight of the Jews in the Shoah that drove him to fight against injustice, to march with Martin Luther King, to rage against what he called the evil of indifference. Just this past week, I visited the Begin center in Jerusalem. Begin, who like Heschel survived World War II, was – unlike Heschel – hardly a name associated with left-leaning causes. Which is why I was fascinated to discover that his very first act as Prime Minister of Israel was to send a ship to pick up 66 Vietnamese refugees whose boat had foundered. Twelve other ships, from twelve other countries, were in the area and ignored them, but Begin, who lived through a world without empathy, when given the opportunity, chose to use his position of power to perform a grand act of human concern.

It may be human to be indifferent, but it is contrary to everything our tradition teaches. Our Torah reading this morning is clear as day on this front. If you want to know how a person should walk through a world where evil exists and persists you need look no further than our Torah reading:

ED: >
Should this be an extract?

> "If you see your fellow's ox or sheep gone astray, do not ignore it. You must take it back to your fellow … You shall do the same with anything that your fellow loses and you find: You must not remain indifferent." (Deut. 22:1–4)

These verses aren't just about lost property; they are an ethical code of conduct for us all, legislation cautioning us against the willful denial of social responsibility. Our sacred tradition teaches us at every turn – from Cain's abdication of moral responsibility in asking God, "Am I my brother's keeper?" to the sin of indifference in the generation of the Tower of Babel, to Joseph's brothers standing before their father and holding the bloodstained tunic in their hands – that a posture of indifference is contrary to who we are meant to be. There is even a Yiddish idiom to describe how we should not behave: *machen sich nit wissendik*, "to pose as unknowing" – to feign ignorance, to be a bystander, to stand idly by. In a sense, our entire code of ethics can be distilled down to the contemporary catchphrase "If you see something, say something."

Certainly in a post-9/11 world we are no longer, if we ever were, allowed to turn a blind eye. Our security, physical and moral, is contingent on a heightened awareness of the sea of our shared humanity. We are obligated to express concern beyond ourselves, we must orient ourselves towards each other, those we know and those we don't. This is the response to a post 9/11 world – a Jewish response, but really a response for all humanity. *Lo tukhal l'hitalem*, "you must not remain indifferent." This is the only path forward in a post-9/11 world.

One of the most identifiable ritual acts of the Jewish people is breaking a glass at the end of a wedding. Tradition teaches that the act reminds us, even at the height of our joy, that we must recall the moments of destruction – the shattered glass strewn over our past, each fragment representing an historic act of indifference. And the couple, who have declared abiding concern for each other, take a courageous step over those broken shards, as if to say, "We see the indifference and we choose to respond, to march forward in the only way, the most powerful way we can, with empathy, love, and mutual concern."

On this tenth anniversary of 9/11, we see the broken shards, the shattered lives, the evil that continues to linger and present itself. And yet we step forward, we step over, courageously, cautiously and, most of all, filled with love, concern, and empathy for our common humanity, all of us created equally in the image of God.

"*If I Forget Thee, O Jerusalem*"

In terms of Biblical prooftexts for supporting Israel, some of the most famous are found in today's Torah and *haftarah* reading. *L'ma'an tziyon lo eḥeshe, u-l'ma'an yerushalayim lo eshkot*, "For the sake of Zion I will not be silent, for the sake of Jerusalem, I will not be still." (Isa. 62:1), and *Al ḥomotayikh yerushalayim hifkadeti shomrim – kol ha-yom v'kol ha-lailah tamid lo yeḥeshu*, "Upon your walls, O Jerusalem, I have set watchmen who shall never be silent by day or by night." (Isa. 62:6). Not in the *parashah*, but probably the most famous of all, sung at weddings and other occasions, comes from the book of Psalms: *Im eshkaḥekh yerushalayim, tishkaḥ yemini*. "If I forget thee, O' Jerusalem, let my right hand wither. Let my tongue cling to the roof of my mouth if I do not remember you, if I do not exalt Jerusalem above my chief joy." (Ps. 137) If you have ever been in my office, then you know that sitting proudly on my wall is a painting by one of my favorite contemporary Israeli artists, Deganit Blechner. In the background is a scene from Jerusalem, and in the foreground appears, among other verses, this verse from Psalm 137, the foundational text for keeping Israel in our hearts and deeds.

Last week my daughter stopped by my office. She looked up at the wall and I could see her sounding out the words on the painting. Then she turned around and asked, "Hey Dad – what happens if you are a lefty?" Does that mean you should say 'Let my left hand wither?' Or do you still say 'Let my right hand wither' – but it's not so bad, because after all, you are a lefty?"

I can't make this stuff up. But after a week like this one, my daughter's question was not only funny, but also eerily prescient and pressingly urgent. We have all been thinking and reading about Israel. My remarks this morning were written uncomfortably, knowing that every day, every hour, brings new news, here in the UN and of course, the reverberations back in the Middle East.

We are one congregation, a congregation filled with righties and lefties. And all of us promise to never forget Jerusalem. When it comes to the challenges facing Israel, I have discovered over the past few years that that my congregation is filled with righties and lefties who share very little – except for the fact none of you are shy, and each of you believes that if only someone in power would listen to you, or to that columnist on the listserv that you keep forwarding to me, then all of Israel's problems would be solved. We are a diverse congregation, no question, but there is something important we share – right or left, all of us promise never to forget our commitment, all of us promise to stand by Israel.

When it comes to Israel's covenantal expectations, the *parashah* describes a remarkably inclusive community. It ranges from the tribal heads and the officials to the woodchopper and the water drawer, those who are present and those who are yet to be present. The Israel tent has always been very large, and is meant to be able to hold a diversity of opinions. There is absolutely no reason to expect or aspire towards a monolithic community. When it comes to Israeli politics, it strikes me as quite reasonable to believe that the opinions in the Diaspora should be as diverse as, well, as diverse as they are in Israel – ranging from the far left to the right. It is an altogether legitimate position to believe that peace will only come by supporting the policies of the left. It is also altogether legitimate to believe that peace will only come by supporting the policies of the right. The pro-Israel, pro-peace tent is very wide and should remain so. This synagogue should be a meeting place for the pro-Israel community from all vantage points.

Truth be told, it is not the right or the left that troubles me, but a third group, more pernicious, and potentially on the rise. One voice that has no place in the dialogue and that defines the limits for our community. The most threatening voice addressing Israel from within the Jewish world is the voice of apathy. It is fascinating to me that the *parashah* explains that a breach of the covenant occurs not when someone thinks thoughts counter to another, rather a breach occurs when someone regards himself immune, thinking "I shall be safe and I will walk in my own willful heart." (Deut 29:18). That person, the Torah explains, the one who disassociates himself from the community, as does the wicked child at the Passover *Seder* table, loses his or her right to be part of the so called peace tent. An evildoer is not a person who thinks differently than you. According to the commentaries, an evildoer, the one who can cause the destruction of the people, is a person who seeks to enjoy the privileges of the community without fulfilling the duties and obligations that come with it. You may not, never ever, separate yourself from Israel. Right or left, I dare not forget thee.

All too often, the complexity of Israel's predicament freezes people into inertia or apathy. As I mentioned, our *haftarah* contains one of the most famous statements about Israel. "Upon your walls, O Jerusalem, I have set watchmen, who shall never be silent by day or by night." Left or right, the litmus test for being pro-Israel is to set watchmen on her walls – in other words – to be concerned about her security. If I can share one criticism of the political left, it is that too often they confuse ambivalence about Israel's internal policies with ongoing concern over Israel's existential security – as if they are mutually exclusive. And If I can share one criticism of the political right, it is that they refuse to find fault in Israel, for fear that in doing so, they will be perceived as being soft on Israel's existential security. I get it, everything is connected and we need to be careful about what we say in public and private. But I honestly don't understand when it became such a complex thought to say I really disagree with what is happening in East Jerusalem, but I am deeply concerned about the threat from Iran and the terrorist network it supports. Remember Rabin? In the early 1990s Rabin deported 415 Islamic fundamentalists to Southern Lebanon. At very same time he was engaged in multilateral negotiations across the Arab world. He knew that one can negotiate peace in earnest while fiercely protecting Israel's interests. The desire for a strong and secure Israel and the desire for Israel to live in peace are not opposite principles – they are actually interdependent. As another verse states, *Adonai oz l'amo yiten, Adonai y'varekh et amo va-shalom.* "God will give strength to Israel and God will bless Israel with peace." It is possible to fight for Israel and for peace at the same time; in fact, it is unconscionable to do otherwise.

It is simply not an option to fancy yourself immune from what Israel is facing. Right or left, you have to step up and get involved. I am reminded of Henry David Thoreau, who in 1846 refused to pay taxes to support government policies to which he objected and was famously thrown into jail. As the story goes, Thoreau's friend Ralph Waldo Emerson came to pay a visit to the jail. Emerson thought Thoreau's actions and subsequent imprisonment were pointless and asked, "Henry, what are you doing in there?" Thoreau replied, "Waldo, the question is, what are you doing out there?" Emerson missed the point of Thoreau's protest. For Thoreau it was inconceivable that he could be party to policies with which he did not agree. The challenge to Emerson – the challenge to all of us – is, given that we are "out here," how exactly are we engaging with the pressing issues of the day?

We are living through a period of seismic shifts when it comes to Israel. In the past six months every geopolitical assumption about the Middle East has been turned upside down. We've seen the storming of the Israeli Embassy in Egypt, the showdown with Turkey, the machinations of the international community. I will be the first to admit that I do not understand everything … and I definitely do not know where and when this rollercoaster ride will slow down. But I do know that when it comes to Israel, it is not an option to sit out a round. At this auspicious time in our people's history we dare not shirk our responsibility. All of us have skin in the game. As the slogan goes: "Wherever we stand, we stand with Israel."

I shared a story of my daughter; let me share a story of my father. June, 1967 marked the outbreak of the Six Day War. My father had just passed his boards as a surgeon and was employed in a London Hospital. As some of you may recall, the mood was somber and dire. Nasser had closed the Straits of Tiran, the UN removed its emergency force in the Sinai, the Jordanians signed a pact with Egypt, and the Syrians were amassing troops in the Golan. I have read my grandfather's sermons from that time – the world really thought this could be the end of Israel. The then Chief Rabbi of England, Immanuel Jakobovits, called for a massive Israel solidarity rally at the Royal Albert Hall in the center of London. Tens of thousands turned out, my father included. Rabbi Jakobovits, who later became a life peer in 1998, made it very clear that the survival of the Jewish people was on the line and he asked everyone to do one of three things. One: If you can go to Israel, get on a plane and go help the Jewish state defend itself. Two: If you can't go – if your personal, professional or familial priorities don't allow you to go – then look after the interests of a person who is going; make sure their business or job is still present when they return. Three: If you can't do either "one" or "two," then give money to support those who are best able to protect Israel's interests.

At the time, Israel needed three professions above all others: truck drivers, anesthesiologists, and surgeons. As a surgeon, my father got on the first plane to Israel. It was the third day of the war. My father tells the story that as they were arriving over the Mediterranean, two Israeli fighter jets escorted them. Upon landing, the passengers discovered that Abba Eban had been on the plane, having just pleaded Israel's case in front of the UN. But my father still thinks the fighter jets were for him, the volunteer surgeon. That summer, my father worked in Israeli hospitals performing skin grafts, reconstructions, and other trauma-related surgeries, often filling in for an Israeli physician who was serving on the front line. My dad's story is just one story, one story of thousands – and nothing in comparison to those who made and continue to make the supreme sacrifice: those who give their lives on behalf of Israel's defense. But I have always had that story tucked away somewhere and, I imagine that my father – who later that fall got married and started his family – always had it tucked away somewhere too. The knowledge that when the going got tough, when Israel needed him, he was there, he responded, he gave what he knew and, along with the rest of the Jewish and world community, helped Israel continue the miracle of its existence.

The year is 2011. It is a different time. The threats of today are different than 1967, different than 1948, different than 1973. But I do believe that no differently than at those moments we are living through a time of transformation, of threat and, please God, of opportunity for Israel. I don't have a crystal ball, and I don't know what is the fastest road to peace. But I do know this. That one day, 10, 20, 30 years from now, we will look back on this moment – just as we look back on '48, '67, '73 – and we will know that we lived through an era when history turned on a pivot. Our children and grandchildren will read about it in a history book and they will walk into our rooms and say, "Dad, Mom – what did you do for Israel then?"

You may or may not be a doctor able to fly to Israel and, for that matter, that may not be what Israel needs right now. You may or may not be in a position to write a check, or sit on a board of some pro-Israel organization. But if you have never gone to a rally, shown support, taken a class, educated yourself, educated a colleague, well let me tell you, this is New York City; the fault is yours. Speak to your children about Israel, travel there, send them for a summer, for a gap year. Build a loving, caring, and nurturing relationship with Israel. It is not in the heavens; it depends only on you. What can I do? My father has a working answer to the question. He gave of himself at the critical hour, so that Israelis could defend the Jewish homeland. Me, you can be sure I personally will have a working answer to that question. And as your rabbi, I can assure you that in this synagogue we will be at the front line of the question. As for you – you have skin in this game. You need an answer to the question of what you did when Israel needed you most.

Right or left. I don't care. Just do not think yourself immune from the Jewish people, do not write yourself out of your covenantal responsibility. Do not look back at this moment and say, "I did nothing."

"If I forget thee, O' Jerusalem, let my right hand wither" … if I cease to think of thee, if I do not keep you in my memory, in my thoughts, and in my deeds at all times.

Erev Rosh Hashanah
"The Stories We Write"

As we greet the New Year, I want to welcome each and every one of you. May we all be inscribed in the Book of Life for a year of health and happiness. For me, this Rosh Hashanah is especially sweet as, for the very first time, I get to welcome both my parents and my in-laws to celebrate Rosh Hashanah together. Mom, Dad, Mom, Dad – I didn't choose any of you, nor for that matter did you choose me. But if I were to do it all again, I would pick all four of you any day.

So with everyone present, I ask your indulgence as I share an observation about my extended family with you, my congregational family. If you were to walk into any of our homes, here in New York, in Pittsburgh, or in Los Angeles, on each of our coffee tables you would find a wedding album – photographs documenting the day Debbie and I got married. That said, if you were to review the albums closely, you would discover, as I did, something very interesting about them – namely, that each album tells a very different story. Let me explain. If you were to look at the New York edition, you would find that the first page is a photograph of our wedding invitation, followed by a picture of Debbie, and then one of me. This is followed by pictures of our families, Debbie and me under the *huppah*, the party, concluding with a parting shot of the happy couple. Now, if you went to Pittsburgh to see the album at my in-laws, you would begin with a picture of Debbie, then Debbie and her mother, then Debbie and her siblings, then her grandmother, and eventually around page six, in a group shot, you see me – the groom. The rewriting of history is no less startling at my parents' home in Los Angeles. There the album begins of course with the primary male/female relationship, the groom and his mother, followed by the mother and the father of the groom, and then me with my brothers, and only then do you catch sight of a wedding crasher dressed in a white gown, who upon closer examination looks a lot like the mother of my four children. And so it is throughout. The Los Angeles album features only my hometown rabbi, any references to Pittsburgh clergy have been expurgated. In the Pittsburgh album, one would never know that there were any guests who were not born in that great rectangular state of Pennsylvania.

As I thought about these albums, I was struck by their differences, which will – at the very least – make for lively dinner conversation in my home later this evening. It is fascinating, really. I am positive we were all at the same wedding and yet, there exist very different records of the event. Each album tells a different story, each constructs a different reality. Each family had the identical set of pictures to choose from and in each book, the order, the emphasis, the beginnings, and the endings lead to very different narratives of that wonderful day.

This evening begins Rosh Hashanah and with it the Days of Awe – the most sacred time of the Jewish year. If there is one image associated with Rosh Hashanah, one constant graphic, visual image, it is that of a book. *L'shanah tovah tikatevu*, we say to each other. "May you be inscribed in the book for a good year." *B'sefer ḥayyim brakhah v'shalom*, we chant. "In the book of life for blessing and peace." Again and again, the tradition returns to the evocative image of a book sitting open before God with pages filled with the stories of our lives, drafted by our own hand, the narratives of who we are.

And so this evening, just as we have opened our *maḥzorim*, I want you to imagine yourself opening the book of your own life, to consider the events, the actions, the proceedings that have made you who you are today. I want you to engage in that divinely inspired task of composing the narrative of your life up to now and for the year to come. Our task is as exciting as it is awe inspiring, to compose our own stories – personal, professional, national – past and future.

You see, the events of our lives arguably have an element of objectivity. They are the proofs, if you will, distributed by the wedding photographer. The manner in which we compose and tell our stories, however, is anything but objective; it is entirely up to us. As human beings, we are inveterate storytellers. And there is no story we like telling more than our own: how we chose our profession, how we met our loved ones, how we became the people that we are today. Consider your own personal mythologies that you have generated over the years. The pivotal conversation that changed the course of your life, that teacher who made you rethink your career path. That job you didn't get way back when, but how it was the other job that opened up so many new doors. I, for example, am often asked how it is I decided to be a rabbi. I have told the story enough to recognize that I have a very specific way of doing so. I know the story so well that I can almost predict where I will pause and inflect. But this predictability does not mean our stories are canned. Rather they are our personal canons, palimpsests upon which the rest of our lives are composed. We all have stories we tell of ourselves and of each other – repeatedly. These stories reflect how we see ourselves and how we want to be seen by others. Cognitive scientists have long noted that our identities are constructed through an endless series of micro-narratives, which we eventually abstract into an overarching macro-narrative of our lives that selects certain plot features by which we build our sense of ourselves – as individuals, as families, and as a nation.

Even the question of where we begin and end our stories is far from a value-free decision. "A beginning is an artifice," wrote Ian McEwan in his novel *Enduring Love*, "And what recommends one over another is how much sense it makes of what follows." The very first comment on the Bible by the great medieval Jewish commentator Rashi alerts us to the importance of beginnings and endings. He asks why, if the point of the Torah is to teach the *mitzvot*, the commandments, does it begin with the universal story of the Garden of Eden? Shouldn't it rather begin with Chapter 12 of Exodus, the first legal section of the Torah? The same question could be asked of the ending of the Torah, which leaves the Children of Israel on the banks of the Jordan, not yet having entered the Promised Land. This oddity so perplexed scholars that, for one period in Biblical scholarship, the Torah was referred to not as the Pentateuch, but as the Hexateuch, with the book of Joshua included as the sixth book. After all, how could the Torah possibly end without a record of the conquest of Canaan? The truth is that the answers to these questions – why the Torah begins with a theme of universal significance and concludes with a destiny unfulfilled – are perhaps the very forces that have shaped the contours of the Jewish conscience and the Jewish condition for thousands of years.

Whether it is the Torah, the Passover *Haggadah* or the events of our lives, where we begin and where we end, what we put in and what we leave out is, in fact, the key to our identities. How we choose to organize and assimilate our experiences into story form is both our greatest challenge and our greatest responsibility. Each of us is given the choice – every day, but never more than over the High Holy Days – of how to craft our narratives. Each of us is given the choice of whether we live our stories or whether our stories live us. Are you an active author of your story, or do you passively allow your story to be written for you? Far too often, for far too many of us, our authorial hand slips. The events we choose to draw from are destructive, and the blessings in our life, overlooked.

I look around this room and I see a million snapshots – many, thank God, joyous ones – births, weddings, *b'nei mitzvah*, and weekday moments of joy. But we have also come to share many sad occasions, some public and some deeply private. The pain of divorce, of infertility, of personal or professional setbacks, for you and often for your children. There are many in our midst who are coping with loss, failure, grief of some kind. People have been betrayed, hurt, injured. Yes, there are probably some things in this world that are beyond forgiveness, and sometimes there are no words to soothe the pain. But in every case, in the wake of every sorrow, at some point, a person must ask himself or herself whether that loss will become the central defining moment of one's life? Will you be so consumed by disappointment that you will be plagued with a perpetually wounded sensibility? It is the very power of crafting our narrative that is often our undoing. We spotlight certain events and ignore others. We emphasize or overlook according to a calculus that may in fact be entirely harmful to our own self-understanding and detrimental to our future. Far too often it is our inability to look beyond present heartache that results in our being immobilized in our pain. We become stuck in the moment – the pages of the album jammed together, unable to flip forward.

On this day of Rosh Hashanah, we commit ourselves with renewed vigilance to the stories we write and the stories we live. It is not merely coherence that we seek; rather we seek to organize the facts of our lives in a way that can strengthen and not weaken, that is truthful but not demoralizing. The facts are the facts, and there is no changing them, but the stories we tell determine who we are and who we will come to be.

I began by speaking of my parents and I will leave you by sharing something of my children. When one of my children was born in Chicago, it was, for a period of time, touch and go. The fact that none of you have any idea which one of my children I am speaking about is an indicator that this story, unlike that of many parents, has a truly happy ending, or more accurately – a happy beginning. And yet, to the day I die, I will never forget that month of my life, sitting in the pediatric ICU with my newborn child, as my kid fought for life, and life and reality came to a screeching halt for me and Debbie as our entire universe was hanging by a thread.

I will never forget the advice given by our pediatrician one morning as our child's health began to improve and we were finally being released into the world with a child whose condition would demand, for the foreseeable future, constant vigilance, frequent check-ups, and regimented medication. We were all well aware of the uncertain road ahead when the doctor pulled me aside and said, "Elliot – you have a choice. You can consider yourself the parent of a child trapped in a condition, or you can choose to see yourself as the parent of a beautiful kid, a parent who, like any other parent, sooner or later discovers that no child is created perfect and every child has his or her own hurdles." "Either way," he continued, "you will be just as vigilant, just as caring, and just as careful; but make no mistake, it will be this choice that will determine everything about your family's future."

It is this lesson, this sage advice given to me by my child's physician, that is the crux of the task before us this evening. Do not take lightly the pivotal events of your life. Now is not the time to gloss over the moments of profound pain and joy that have collectively made us who we are. We must be responsive, we must be reflective. Yet the gift of Rosh Hashanah is to be able to see our life story in a new light, through different eyes, and with a renewed vision. Step by step we need to lift ourselves out of the dungeon of determinism and allow for our stories to be rewritten. We are free to recreate ourselves, empowered to shatter the bars that imprison us. The facts are the facts, but the stories we write, the narratives we bring before God, that we pass down to future generations, are ultimately our own to compose.

L'shanah tovah tikatevu. May we all be written in the Book of Life for a year of health, life, and peace.

Rosh Hashanah
"Waiting for a Miracle"

Precisely 70 years ago, on September 29 and 30, 1941, the single most horrific and infamous mass killing of the Holocaust occurred at Babi Yar. It is an altogether sobering thought that during these hours that we gather in our holiday finest, seventy years ago, nearly 34,000 of our people were gathered together in a ravine outside of Kiev, ordered to strip down, made to lie on top of each other, and were then shot by the Nazis and their collaborators. Having marched into the Soviet Union just a few months earlier, the Nazi Einsatzgruppen had turned their focus and function to the Jews, and on those two days an entire Jewish community was efficiently and systematically machine-gunned in a two-day orgy of execution. September 29 and 30, 1941. We remember them every day – especially today, seventy years to the day – and pray that their souls be forever bound up in God's eternal embrace.

Babi Yar you already may have known about. But let me now tell you about what happened exactly twenty years later, in September of 1961. Because it was fifty years ago this month, literally from the very graves of Babi Yar, that one of the greatest stories in our people's history arose.

As recounted by Gal Beckerman in his extraordinary book on the struggle for Soviet Jewry, it was in September of 1961 that the popular and influential newspaper *Literaturnaya Gazeta* published a poem called "Babi Yar," written by a young writer, Yevgeny Yevtushenko.

Yevtushenko had visited Babi Yar only to discover that this ravine, the site of two of the darkest days in human history, had been ingloriously turned into a garbage dump. The first words of Yevtushenko's poem lament: "No monument stands over Babi Yar." Invoking the names of Alfred Dreyfus and Anne Frank, he condemned the anti-Semitism of his compatriots and the whitewashing of Soviet Jewry and he identified with Jewish suffering, concluding: "And I myself am one massive, soundless scream above the thousand thousand buried here. I am each old man here shot dead. I am every child here shot dead. Nothing in me shall ever forget!"

As moving as the poem was, its reverberations were both wider and more unexpected than anyone thought possible. The newspaper containing it immediately sold out. Thousands of students gathered to hear the poem read even as the government tried to squelch it. By April of 1962, Yevtushenko was on the cover of *Time* magazine. Shostakovich, the famed Soviet composer, set the poem to music, and by December 1962, the Moscow Philharmonic first performed the piece.

Beckerman himself would caution us from identifying any single moment as the tipping point in history. But, by one telling, it was from the publication of that poem, fifty years ago this month, that one of the greatest reclamations of Jewish identity in history emerged. After decades of Communism, the horrors of the World War II, and years of Stalin, Jewish identity in what was then the Soviet Union had been thoroughly repressed under totalitarian rule. There was no legal way to teach Hebrew, no circumcision, no rituals of any kind. Jewish life had been physically and spiritually gutted.

The miraculous struggle of Soviet Jewry was not merely the story of Natan Sharansky, the *refuseniks*, the protests and legislation that led to the release of millions of prisoners of conscience. The miracle of Soviet Jewry was that, against all odds, a community with the most tenuous connection to its roots – with every reason not to be Jewish, to forget their identity – remembered that they were Jews. In remembering, they heroically insisted on wresting their Jewishness back from the clutches of oblivion. The secret reading groups, the Hebrew classes, the production and distribution of *samizdat*, underground Jewish literature, the thousands of American Jews (perhaps some in this room) who participated in and supported daring and dangerous efforts to provide Soviet Jewry with a lifeline to its Jewish identity – the story of Soviet Jewry was a story of "Let my people go!" But it was also a story of "Let my people know!" Were it not for this retrieval of Jewish identity against all odds, I don't think it is an understatement to say that the second, more public, story of release never would have happened.

I was raised on these stories, although because I was young, for my first few protest marches, I thought I was marching for Soviet "Jewelry," not "Jewry." But it was with these stories in mind that I traveled on a UJA mission to the FSU this past summer with John Ruskay, Natan Sharansky, and New York rabbinical colleagues. Twenty years since the collapse of the Soviet Union, years after the emigration of over one million Jews to Israel and America, what would Soviet Jewry look like? At long last able to practice freely what couldn't be practiced for decades, able to live openly as Jews – this was something I had to see with my own eyes.

Much to my surprise, I discovered that Russian Jewry looks an awful lot like the American Jewry I see every day. We visited synagogues and campus Hillels, we saw Holocaust Museums and JCC's, we saw Jewish summer camps – we saw the sacred mission of JAFI, JDC, and UJA-Federation being actualized every day. We met with the young people in St. Petersburg who produced a YouTube Purim song to the Black-Eyed Peas, not unlike last year's Hanukkah hit song set to the melody of Tai Cruz's "Dynamite." We saw gorgeous Jewish institutions that lacked for nothing on the same day we visited food pantries cutting back on their Jewish clientele for lack of sufficient funds. We met Reform rabbis complaining about Chabad rabbis and Chabad rabbis complaining about Reform rabbis, and we met upscale Moscow families boxing each other out to get into the JCC Early Childhood program. In other words, I felt right at home.

But more than the institutional similarities, what I was surprised to discover was that Russian Jewry and American Jewry have one essential feature in common. They both lack memory. I am hard pressed to think of two communities that experienced the twentieth century in more dissimilar ways. And yet the cultural consequence of living under the radical democracy and freedoms of America and the extreme totalitarianism of Soviet Russia are ironically the same. In both contexts memory has been wiped clean and cultural amnesia has set in. The great American writer Henry Miller once said about travel: "One's destination is never a place, but rather a new way of looking at things." The "aha" moment of my Russian experience was the discovery that they, like us, are constructing Jewish identity on a *tabula rasa*. Like the story this past summer about the famous baseball player Ralph Branca who woke up one day to discover that he had been Jewish all along, contemporary Jewry – Russian, American, and otherwise – are stumbling onto their Jewish identities, oblivious to the past investments and sacrifices of those who came before.

I am reminded of the sharp joke told of the rabbi leaving synagogue after *Kol Nidre* services. On his way home he was astonished to see Goldstein, one of his congregants, sitting in a non-kosher restaurant and eating a sumptuous meal. The rabbi was furious and waited for Goldstein to finish eating and pay for the meal. As Goldstein exited the restaurant the rabbi accosted him: "Goldstein, What are you doing, I just saw you eating *treif*, and paying for it on Yom Kippur. Explain yourself!" Goldstein replied, "Oy, I am sorry, Rabbi, but I just forgot." "What do you mean? Did you forget that today was Yom Kippur?" "No." "Did you forget that it is forbidden to eat and drink on Yom Kippur?" "No." "Did you forget that it is forbidden to eat non-kosher food?" "No." "Goldstein, tell me, what is it that you forgot?" "Rabbi, for a moment, I forgot I was a Jew." We have become, to adopt the language of A.B. Yehoshua, *Yehudim asher shakhahu she-hem yehudim*, "Jews who have forgotten that they are Jews."

Jonathan Safran Foer once wrote that Jews have not five, but six senses – the sixth being memory. Memory is the fiber that binds one generation to another as a community. It is our ability to recall our past – historical and mythical – that binds us as a people. So, too, as individuals. Not unlike the experience of Proust, who once explained that his biting into a buttery madeleine cookie triggered a powerful series of associations from his youth, the sounds, tastes, and sensations of Jewish practice trigger the *yiddishkeit* submerged within each of us and in many cases link us to the arc of our identity that preceded our own individual existence. These associations are planted within us all, the substrata of our identities for which we owe an immeasurable debt of gratitude to those who came before us.

But here is the rub. While we are who we are owing to the seeds planted by prior generations, there is absolutely nothing cumulative about the construction of Jewish identity. It is a bit like my marriage – it doesn't matter that I changed that light bulb last week – the only question that matters is when am I going to put that piece of luggage back in the storage locker! Yes, the practices of your grandparents and parents are important to you, as they should be, but that doesn't mean they resonate the same way with your children and grandchildren. I don't say this lightly, proudly, or with any joy; it is deeply painful to concede that there is no inherited disposition to associate with a synagogue, give to UJA, marry Jewish, or engage in other Jewish activities. But the only thing worse would be to assume that there is. Even in Israel, Jewish identity has been superseded by nationalism; for many secular Israelis the *tallit* has been replaced by the Israeli flag. Whether it is New York, St. Petersburg, or Tel Aviv, the assumed, mimetic modes of transmitting identity from one generation to the next are simply no longer in play. Our situation is like the scene in the classic novel *One Hundred Years of Solitude*, where Gabriel Garcia Marquez tells of an entire village in which people are afflicted with forgetfulness, a contagious sort of amnesia. One young man, still unaffected, tries to limit the damage by labeling everything. "This is the table," "This is the window," "This is a cow, it has to be milked every morning." All Jews have become, in a sense, Jews who have forgotten that they are Jews.

In 2011, we do not stand on the rubble of Communism, nor on the shallow graves of Babi Yar. We are living through what will forever be known as the freest, most prosperous, and most blessed moment of Jewish history – period! And yet if we are to arrive fifty years from now in strength, we will need a miracle as momentous and unexpected as that of Soviet Jewry. We need, as it were, a Marshall plan to restore Jewish memory to contemporary Jewry. Don't forget that it is on the pivot of memory that every single redemptive moment of our people has occurred. It was when God remembered Noah that the flood waters subsided; when Joseph remembered his dreams that he began to reconcile with his brothers; when God remembered Israel that the redemption from Egypt began; and when Mordecai was remembered by Ahasuerus that the Jews of Persia were saved. The reason the rabbis give for why we read the Torah reading we do on Rosh Hashanah is that God *remembered* Sarah. For Jews the act of rebirth and renewal are tied into the act of remembering. Today, a day of new beginnings, is called *Yom HaZikaron* – the day of memory. The *maḥzor* refers to God as *Zokher kol hanishkaḥot* – A God who "remembers all the forgotten things." It is incumbent upon us to draw on this divine quality, to commit ourselves to remembering, to remembering even what has been forgotten.

This synagogue – and really all institutions of contemporary Jewish life – needs to recalibrate our mission with the knowledge that unless we are culturally competitive, we are dead in the water. Ours is an age of Sisyphean spirituality, in which the rock of Jewish identity is rolled up the hill in every generation, only to roll back again so the next generation must take up the task once more. Our schools, our services, our programming, our everything needs to recognize that every would-be Jew has the choice of what and how to practice. As the *Haggadah* makes clear, *b'khol dor va-dor*, in every generation, one must construct and reconstruct Jewish identity. It is at our own peril that we ignore the fact that Jewish life exists in the marketplace of ideas. But such an awareness does not mean lowering a bar, rather just the opposite – it means we insist, more than ever, that the product we create must burst forth with creativity, authenticity, and excellence. The most successful programs on the Jewish scene right now – Birthright, PJ Library, AJWS, Chabad, to name a few – provide authentic, compelling, and engaging Jewish content knowing full well that participants will vote with their feet, drawn in by excellence, and turned off by mediocrity. The Jewish institutions that are suffering are those that are operating on a business-as-usual model, working on assumptions of past affiliation that are neither compelling nor accessible to contemporary Jews. I promise that in this synagogue every single day, every single staff person we hire, every single dollar we raise, will serve the urgent and burning need to create dynamic Jewish life for passion-filled Jews. We will leave it all out on the field, we will not submit to the tyranny of mediocrity, we will give every searching Jew the most valuable and countercultural gift we know. We will give you the gift of memory upon which you can build your Jewish future.

That is what we will do, what I commit to today and every day I show up for work. But let me tell you – it is not enough. I need to ask you to do the same. I need you to see your mission as being a generator of Jewish memory. Not just today, or at the *Seder* table, but as the single most important act you can do as a Jew. When you take your children to Israel, what you are doing is creating memory. When you light Shabbat candles in your home, you are creating memories. When you come into this synagogue and follow the Torah reading with your grandchildren sitting next to you, they will have that forever. When you hear yourself, your child, or your grandchild humming the cantor's melodies after you have left the building, then you have created Jewish memory. It is an investment that may not yield a return until you and I are long gone. But this is your time and if you don't do it, nobody else will. That is what our predecessors did for us and that is what we must do for those who follow.

I began with a story of Russian Jewry and it is with that I would like to leave you. For me, the most moving stop of last summer's trip was a visit to the Moscow Choral Synagogue. When the tour bus arrived, I immediately went upstairs to the women's section wanting to see what is, perhaps, the most famous synagogue seat in Russian Jewish history. You may recall that in the darkest days of Soviet Jewry, Golda Meir went to the Soviet Union to serve as the ambassador for the fledgling State of Israel. A savvy politician, Golda understood timing. Though no announcement had been made, the public intuitively assumed that the Israeli ambassador would attend holiday services. Golda came to the synagogue on Rosh Hashanah, and the Jews came, too. They kept coming and coming until the crowd – estimated at between thirty and fifty thousand Jews – overflowed into the streets. The synagogue was filled to capacity; there was no room to stand, no space to yield. The women in the balcony kept approaching Golda to kiss her hand, touch her arm. As Israel's military attaché was called to the Torah, walking proudly in his *yarmulke* emblazoned with an Israeli flag, so many tears flowed that the service came to a halt. Eventually, the shofar blew for a final time, and Golda stood up to leave, overwhelmed by the weight of her own emotions. As the crowd saw her move, they erupted in Hebrew, Russian, and Yiddish, *Golda Shelanu, Nasha Golda, Goldele undser Golda*, at which point a voice cried out the opening strains of *Hatikvah*. The crowd was filled with such emotion that Golda's security had to usher her out. And at that final moment, Golda finally found her voice. She turned to the crowd and said in Yiddish: *A dank eich vos ihr seit geblieben yiden.* "Thank you … for having remained Jews."

I sat there last summer, in Golda's seat, thinking about that fateful Rosh Hashanah, thinking about the tens of thousands and I suppose millions of Jews who possessed only the most inchoate Jewish memories, the most meager reasons to stay connected. And yet they did, they chose to remain Jews, they remembered when they could have forgotten, and they built on those memories, and their story went on to become the greatest Jewish story ever told.

It is Rosh Hashanah 2011 – seventy years since Babi Yar, fifty years since the struggle for Soviet Jewry began – and I am yearning for another miracle. Whether it happens or not – whether fifty years from now our descendents will look back to thank us – that is for me, that is for you, that is for all of us to decide. Today, may we commit to making the right decision, to remember, to build – and may we be remembered as builders of a glorious Jewish future.

"A Complaint is a Gift"

Next time you are on Lexington Avenue, I want you to stop to appreciate the beautiful church that sits between 75th and 76th – the church of St. Jean Baptiste. Over the past few years, I have attended a variety of interfaith meetings there, not to mention dropping my children off at the Broadway Babies program hosted in their auditorium.

Whether or not you have ever been inside, I am guessing you do not know the incredible story of how the building was built. The church has been around for hundreds of years, one of the oldest in New York. It was historically a humble structure, a far cry from the fancier churches closer to the Fifth Avenue mansions. As the story goes, one Sunday in 1910, Thomas Fortune Ryan, a prominent Roman Catholic financier, arrived a bit late for high mass. The church was over-crowded, bursting at the seams – standing room only – and Mr. Ryan had to stand for the duration of the service. After mass, Mr. Ryan approached Father Letellier, complaining about what had happened, insistent that the church was too small to accommodate all its parishioners. Father Letellier listened intently, absorbing his congregant's displeasure, but he was also not a man to fumble and stumble. When Mr. Ryan pressed to know what it would take to build a new church, the Father responded: "not a penny less than $300,000." Mr. Ryan replied at once "Very well, have your plans made up and I will pay for the church." And so it was. Mr. Ryan, a disgruntled congregant, went on to become the benefactor of one of the most beautiful churches on the Upper East Side, if not all of New York City.

It is an amazing story, all the more amazing because it is true, told to me not long ago by the present pastor of the church. A story of how a complaint was turned to a gift – it is actually something that happens more often than you might think. I just received an email from the alumni association of my alma mater, the University of Chicago. It told a story that you may have seen reported in the paper – the story of Carolyn Bucksbaum, who bristled at the arrogant physician who brusquely dismissed her intuition about her ailment. She turned out to be right; the doctor was wrong and the doctor never even bothered to apologize. Mrs. Bucksbaum came to believe that as much as they must master the science of medicine, physicians should also learn compassion and empathy, in other words, bedside manner. And so it was that last week, the University of Chicago found itself on the receiving end not of a complaint, but a gift – to the tune of $42 million – for the establishment of the Bucksbaum Institute for Clinical Excellence.

For reasons that are not difficult to figure out, I love these stories of complaints being transformed into gifts. But no week more than this one, on *Shabbat Shuvah*, the Sabbath of Repentance, are these stories relevant, not in terms of physical gifts, but another kind of gift. The idea that the complaints we receive – for which you and I are so often on the receiving end – difficult as they are to hear, can be understood as gifts towards personal transformation. After all, for the past two days of Rosh Hashanah, every rabbi has told every Jew that this is the week to come clean with those we love most, to communicate openly and honestly about where we must be better; not only that we must be vulnerable about our own shortcomings, but we should forthcoming about what we need from others. In other words, we need to complain! To truly take in the message of the season, we must be willing to give and receive complaints – complaints about each of us.

Now I know what you are thinking. Rabbi, you have got to be kidding me: a complaint is a gift?! Who likes to hear a complaint? Nobody. None of us tends to handle it well when someone complains. The standard response to *kvetchers* is to shut off. We look at the speaker, nodding intently as they tell us what we did wrong; meanwhile, a switch flicks in our head, the shields go up, and like in a Peanuts cartoon, the voice of criticism is transformed into an indistinct "wah, wah, wah." Occasionally, when we are really on our game, we engage in a series of mental gymnastics while the person is complaining to us. We say to ourselves, "Oh, they think they are complaining about me, but this is really about their bad marriage, unhappy job, something that happened in their childhood, or they are just plain nuts." Anything rather than allow for the possibility that their complaint could actually be valid. Most often, when someone complains, we tighten up – physically and emotionally. We feel personally attacked, our temperature rises, we crouch down into a defensive position, and before even hearing the full complaint, we are already working on a vicious response. We hate complaints because we hate to be wrong and we hate all the stuff that comes with being wrong, like being reflective, introspective, apologetic, and experiencing other awkward sentiments we would rather avoid. And the only thing worse than being wrong is someone telling us that we are wrong. Nobody likes complaints and I'll be the first to admit it.

But with all the qualifiers stated, in the spirit of the new year, come with me on a mental experiment, this working hypothesis that, under certain circumstances, complaints can be gifts.

First of all, complaining is in the DNA of our people. From the very moment we left Egypt, the Jewish people have been habitual *kvetchers*. Too much food, too little food, when will get to the Promised Land, when can we go back to Egypt? From Moses, to the Rivers of Babylon, to Gilda Radner's "It's always something," Jews have a rich tradition of perpetual dissatisfaction.

Remember the story of Sadie Goldstein, the Jewish grandmother, who was walking on the beach with her grandson when a huge wave crashed down, sweeping the boy into the depths of the ocean. Sadie dropped to her knees and turned to heaven praying for the return of her grandson. "Please God, I have always been a good person, a good Jew, and a loving grandmother; please return my grandson to me." Just as she is finishing her prayer, another huge wave crashes back returning the young boy to his grandmother's side. Sadie begins to cry and hug the grandson she thought she would never see again. She is overcome with joy and gratitude. She looks once more at her grandson, then looks up at the heavens, and yells, "He had a hat!"

Or what about the story of the four Jewish women sitting on the beach. The first says, "*Oy.*" The second says, "*Oy vey.*" The third says, "*Oy vey'z mir.*" The fourth turns to them and says, "Ladies, I thought we promised not to talk about our children."

It is part of our DNA, the "Oy" chromosome, the subtext of every good Jewish joke. We know it could always be worse, but that doesn't stop us from complaining about how bad it is, about ourselves, and about each other. But like chopped liver and anti-Semitism, just because it's always been around doesn't necessarily make it a good thing. How exactly can it be a good thing to be on the receiving end of a complaint? Let me give you a few reasons.

First, of all, a complaint is an expression of a relationship. I get angry all the time, but I only complain when I care. As Elie Wiesel eloquently stated, "The opposite of love is not hate, it's indifference." If you are mistreated in a store and you can get the product elsewhere, you walk away and take your business with you. So too with people; when you don't care about someone, you write them off. It is only when, for whatever reason, you are invested in continuing a relationship that you bother to complain. I know it is counterintuitive, but next time someone complains to you, think of it in that way. If they didn't care on some level, they wouldn't bother to pick up the phone, confront you about your shortcomings, and let you know where you fell short of expectations. It doesn't make it any easier, and you still may be right and they wrong, but it may enable you to respond to the moment with a more moderated sensibility.

Second, a complaint is important because if someone is complaining, then odds are they are not the only person who feels that way. For a congregational rabbi, this is a critically important rule of thumb. I get complaints all the time, by phone, email, in person, usually at *Kiddush*. And whether I think I am right or wrong, I realize that, whether I am actually right or wrong, there is the bigger question of perception. Our actions are often received in ways that they were never intended. A complaint, well founded or not, is a wake up call, a view into your behavior, of how your words and deeds are being received. You may have seen the exhibit at the Met, the photography of Paul Strand. Strand sought to achieve the greatest possible degree of objectivity in his portraits. So he outfitted himself with a specially fitted camera with a side mount in order to photograph a person without being noticed. So too a complaint. It is not the only angle, but it can serve as a perspective on yourself of which you are unaware. And given the laws of probability, there is more than one person picking up on that same behavior of yours. Remember rule number one: a complaint is a gift because that person cares. Just imagine how many people see that same shortcoming of yours, but because they don't care as much as the person who did bother to complain – they just walked away. Not an easy thought for a rabbi to absorb; for that matter, not an easy thought for anyone to take in.

Third, a complaint is a gift because – drum roll please – that person could actually be right! I know, I know, it is difficult to imagine, but as the expression goes, even a broken clock is right twice a day. We are proud people, we don't like admitting that we are wrong, but at least once a year, during these ten days of Rosh Hashanah and Yom Kippur and the days between, we carry ourselves a little differently, we allow for a bit more humility in our demeanor. Our tone is different, our rush to judgment more cautious. A short while ago, a congregant brought a complaint to me. That person did it thoughtfully, privately, and with love for this institution and great personal regard for me. It was a profoundly moving experience and it continues to be so weeks later. It has forced me to reflect on the incident at hand, and it has forced me to reflect on how I conduct myself in the future. In a very substantive way it has brought me closer to the person, elevated that person in my estimation and, I hope, made me a better human being and a better rabbi. When someone complains in the right way and when you hear it in the right way, a complaint is a tremendous gift and can be the single most important tool we have to create relationships of meaning.

There are lots of reasons, but maybe the simplest one is this. At this time of year, we need to be open to hearing complaints because this is what we ask of God. *Sh'ma koleinu*, "Hear our voices." What are the High Holy Days if not a liturgical expression of the most basic human need to have our voices heard by God. Milton once wrote, "Complaint is the largest tribute Heaven receives." On the High Holy Days we place our tributes at the divine footstool, hopeful that God will be moved by our pleas. How can we possibly ask this kindness of God if we ourselves are not willing to extend the same courtesy to those we love most.

There is a tongue in cheek *midrash*, rabbinic legend, that the reason God instructed the Israelites to build the *mishkan*, the desert tabernacle, was simply because it would give them something to do instead of complaining. Some temples are built to help us avoid complaining; some churches are built because of a fortuitous complaint.

For us, the question during these Days of Repentance is what role complaints will play as we think about the structures we are building in the year to come. One thing I can guarantee you – the complaints will come. Your choice is how you will receive those complaints. This week, try to look at them as gifts, insights into what we don't yet know about ourselves, what we need to know in order to become the people we seek to be.

Yom Kippur
"The Greater Good"

This past year, I had the opportunity to visit the Menachem Begin Museum in Jerusalem. In learning of Begin's legacy, I was fascinated to discover that when asked to identify his greatest achievement, Begin did not mention the signing of the Camp David Peace Accords, the bombing of the Osirak-Iraqi nuclear reactor, his early life surviving the Soviet Gulag, or even his being elected as Prime Minister. Rather, he reflected: "After my death I hope that I shall be remembered, above all, as someone who prevented civil war."

In Begin's mind, his enduring legacy was to be found not in the moments he dug in his feet, but in the instances when he insisted on suppressing his personal politics for a principle greater than himself, which for Begin was a unified Israel. Remember, in pre-state Israel, Begin's Irgun often stood at odds with Ben Gurion's Haganah, which Begin believed to be far too cooperative with the British. Yet, even in the darkest hours, when Irgun-niks were being turned over to the British by the Haganah, a time referred to as "the hunting season," Begin gave orders to his men to restrain themselves – Jews should never shed Jewish blood – *ki yehudim anaḥnu*, because we are Jews. In 1948, at the dawn of Israel's independence, when Ben Gurion declared a state, there was genuine concern that Begin would launch a counter-revolution. Nobody believed Begin would submit to Ben Gurion's authority, and yet it was exactly at that moment that the Irgun emerged from the underground with Begin declaring allegiance to the new government – what Begin called "our government."

Most famously, a month later, in June of 1948, Begin informed those who had been his Zionist adversaries that arms were to be off-loaded on the beach near Kfar Vitkin, north of Tel Aviv. Begin clashed with members of his own Irgun who wanted to keep the arms for themselves, but Begin insisted on the authority of the new Jewish government. He went aboard the ship, the Altalena, in an effort to cool the rising tempers. At that moment, the Palmach fired on the ship in the mistaken belief that Begin and his Irgun comrades were unloading the arms. Standing on the burning deck under fire, coated black from the acrid smoke, Begin yelled frantically to his men, "Don't shoot back! Don't open fire. No civil war." Begin wept openly that night on the radio in a raspy voice affirming "long live the people of Israel." In his autobiography, Begin would later reflect: "There are times when the choice is between tears or blood. Sometimes, as the rebellion against our [British] oppressors taught us, it is necessary for blood to prevail over tears; sometimes, as the Altalena taught us, it is necessary for tears to prevail over blood." Decades would pass and there would be countless moments of victory and defeat in Begin's career. But the moments which he remembered most, the ones for which he wanted to be remembered, were this and perhaps other excruciatingly difficult moments, when he insisted that one principle rise above all others, above his own feelings – in order to serve the greater need of the hour.

Historians, but really all of us, tend to be disinclined to remember such moments, times when we have chosen tears over blood. We are conditioned to believe that heroism comes by way of unflinching adherence to principle, represented by the Gandhis, Martin Luther Kings and Rabbi Akivas of this world who exemplify King's statement that "A man who won't die for something is not fit to live."

And yet, this year, on this Yom Kippur, I am of the opinion that ours is an era calling for a different kind of heroism, a heroism that is sorely lacking in our discourse, from the world at large to the quiet of our homes. A heroism that Begin understood well – based on the conviction that sometimes there is a good greater than one's own, sometimes there is a principle at hand beyond one's self-interest, and sometimes, to paraphrase Begin, you and I must shed tears today, in order that more tears and more blood will not be shed in the years to come.

When we arrive at synagogue on Yom Kippur, we are called upon to look both inward and outward in hope of identifying the fractures and fissures of our lives that are in desperate need of repair. If I had to identify the pathology of our present cultural moment, it would be our collective inability to draw on what Begin and countless other unsung historical figures understood, that at the critical moment one's own truth must, on occasion, give way for a greater good. It is not in vogue; it doesn't make headlines, and it runs absolutely counter to our pervading combative culture of incivility. But if you look at the story lines, here in America, in the Middle East, within Israel, in our own families, then you will see that, in each instance, the defect is one and the same. We have allowed petty self-interest to impede our ability to strive towards the greater good that beckons us.

In his classic work *Civilization and Its Discontents*, Freud explained the root cause of cultures, nations, or religions turning against each other, using the felicitous expression 'the narcissism of minor differences.' It is, he explained, owing to the utter vanity of a people or a person, who, due to their own ego and self-absorption, choose to inflate minor disagreements at the expense of potentially much greater relationships. Our passions and wrath, wrote Montaigne, focus on false and fantastical objects, never those things that are worthy of our attention. We do it all the time in counter-productive and self-destructive ways, insisting that we are acting in defense of principle. But the only thing we are really defending is our ego. We let a minor difference become an impediment eclipsing the totality of the relationship at hand. You may be familiar with the story of two of the greatest artists of the twentieth century, Mondrian and his friend and disciple Theo van Doesburg. Intellectual peers, artistic comrades, true friends, their split and separation came in 1924. Why? Because van Doesburg started to paint diagonal lines rather than the strict horizontal and vertical lines of Mondrian. Two visions – the Elementalism of van Doesburg and Mondrian's Neo-Plasticism – a difference in the angle of a line, a difference that neither man's ego could overcome. (See A. Margalit, *On Compromise*)

We live in a time of cultural pugilism, where self-interest dominates the common interest, where dialogue has devolved into a contact sport. Remember, the reason the rabbis give for the destruction of the Second Temple was not geopolitics, not idolatry, and not immorality, but the sin of *sinat ḥinam*, causeless hatred – the persistent human failing that allows minor differences of opinion to erupt into rancor and factionalism. As in the Dr. Seuss tale about the North-Going Zax and the South-Going Zax, we confront each other with a self-assured swagger, standing face to face, puffed up with pride, while the rest of the world builds around us as we stand unbudging in our tracks. We divide the world between us and them, fetishizing our principles, and demonizing the other, while the temple around us collapses onto the idolatry of our own egos.

There is a story of two Chabadniks who are discussing the Jewish world. One says to the other, "You know, Goldstein, the whole world is divided between us and them – Chabadniks and non-Chabadniks – and there is no point speaking about them. And among us, the world is divided between Ashkenazim and Sephardim – and there is no use talking of the Sephardim. And among us Ashkenazim, there are the Zionists and the non-Zionists – and there is no point in talking about the non-Zionists. And among the Zionists, there are the intellectuals and the non-intellectuals – and there is no use to talking about the latter. And then among the intellectuals, there is just you and me. And Goldstein, we both know how little you know."

At our own peril, we isolate the world into us and them, until we have nobody to speak to but ourselves. As Bill Bishop explains in his book *The Big Sort*, all across America, at every level, there is a dangerous clustering taking place, whereby people exist in their own feedback loop, Balkanized into like-minded communities and separated from each other. On every issue of the day, we have allowed the greater good to be sacrificed on the altars of our own egos.

Today, Yom Kippur, is the day that the healing must begin. Today we try to mend that which has been torn asunder. Today we expand the lens of our perception beyond what we would normally think possible and dream of the world we seek to create. We become bigger people and we seek to eradicate the malignancy that has metastasized throughout our culture. Today we seek to build a year of health – to see the bigger picture – the world we hope to create. Today we know the stakes are greater than any one of us.

As you may know, this fall our synagogue has extended hospitality and classroom space to Ramaz in the wake of their fire over the summer. There is a story told of the Ramaz himself, Rabbi Moshe Zevulun Margolis, who was studying one Friday afternoon right before Shabbat with his grandson-in-law, Rabbi Joseph Lookstein, when a disheveled woman knocked frantically on their door. In her hand was a bag with a chicken in it, and she explained that she believed the chicken to have an imperfection making it *treif*. She insisted that the rabbi check to see if it was kosher. The young Rabbi Lookstein examined the chicken and confirmed that indeed, due to the nature of the blemish, the chicken was *treif*, not fit to eat. The crestfallen woman collected her chicken and began to leave, at which point the older rabbi asked her to wait a moment. He looked at the chicken, walked over to his bookshelf, and with a dramatic flair pulled out a volume. He studied it for some time, replaced the volume, looked once more at the chicken, and said, "I don't like to overrule the young rabbi, but it seems I have found a subtlety of the law that he hadn't considered. It is my studied opinion that indeed the chicken is kosher. The woman walked out. The door closed behind her and Rabbi Lookstein looked at his grandfather, flabbergasted. He couldn't understand what had happened; this one wasn't close, the chicken was as *treif* as it comes. The Ramaz looked at his grandson and said: "Let me explain something to you. That was a poor woman. It is Friday afternoon, the shops are closed; that chicken is what she is serving her family for dinner tonight. If the chicken isn't kosher, the family doesn't eat. The chicken … is kosher."

We all have principles – rules we live by. They are what make us who we are and we dare not become a caricature of Groucho Marx's famous quip: "Those are my principles, if you don't like them, I have others." But in order for this world to exist and new ones to be created, we need to realize that none of us lives in a vacuum. Our own principles – religious, political, and so on – exist in competition with others and, sometimes, for society to exist, we have to find the greater good. The rabbis of the Talmud understood that in a legal tradition like ours, two principles would often find themselves at odds, and it would be incumbent upon us to decide between them. Most famously, *pikuaḥ nefesh*, the requirement to save a life, is an imperative of such importance that even the laws of the Sabbath and Yom Kippur may – if not must – be broken in order to fulfill it. Also well known is the Talmudic discussion of how one should describe a bride on her wedding day. One rabbi, Shammai, says if she is pretty, call her pretty; if she is ugly, tell it like it is. Another rabbi, Hillel, taught that every bride is described as beautiful on her wedding day. For Hillel, truth gives way to a greater good. Not surprisingly, Hillel officiated at a lot more weddings than Shammai.

You will be surprised to discover that you actually already know the technical term for this principle at work. It is *tikkun olam*. I know, you think *tikkun olam* means social justice, repairing the world, or political activism. In its contemporary usage that is what it has come to mean. But in the Talmud itself, *tikkun olam* refers to a very specific legal occurrence when adherence to one principle must give way towards the realization of a greater good. Two quick examples: We are told that one must always pay ransom to redeem captives – an important *mitzvah*, maybe the most important – but the Talmud says a community should never pay too much. Why? Owing to *tikkun olam* – because if we did, kidnappers would have an incentive to capture and demand ransom for even more people. Second example: it is well known that ancient Israel operated on a system of sabbatical release whereby debts were forgiven every seven years. Yet Hillel (the same rabbi who did all the weddings) did away with this institution – for the sake of *tikkun olam* – because the very poor who were supposed to be helped by the release of debts, were, de facto, no longer being lent money. I could give you a dozen more examples. In each case it is for reasons of *tikkun olam* that a law is modified or neutralized – for the sake of a greater concern. Which, if you stop to think about it, is a far more profound way to understand what it means to repair the world than merely doing a good deed. And incidentally, it is what today, Yom Kippur, is all about. After all, if the temple was destroyed for reasons of *sinat ḥinam*, causeless hatred, then wouldn't it make sense that its repair comes by way of *tikkun olam*?

Today, we take a hard long look at all the institutions in which we are invested, our government, our places of work, our synagogue, but none more closely than our own families. If the holidays alert us to one thing, it is that in order for forgiveness to take place, we must see the forest from the trees, we dare not allow ourselves to latch onto any minor shortcoming at the expense of a greater relationship. Sadly, I see it all the time, families torn apart, relatives no longer speaking. More often than not at funerals, the rabbi's office becomes a meeting place for family members who have long since stopped talking to each other. Sisters who because of a slight that nobody quite remembers cannot bring themselves to speak to each other, who even at death, I have discovered, will not attend the other's funeral. I was so struck a few weeks ago to read the story of Steve Jobs, that even when he was facing death, neither he nor his biological father was prepared to pick up the phone to call the other. Presumably a combination of pride, distrust, and past hurt prevented father and son from speaking, an obstinacy that now never will be reconciled.

Yom Kippur reminds us that time is not on our side nor does it heal all wounds. An awareness of our own mortality is meant to serve as the activating agent towards reconciliation. A few weeks ago, I attended *shivah* in the home of a man who had recently lost a brother, leaving the surviving siblings deeply aware that they were the only ones left of their childhood family. Having buried one brother, the remaining brothers sat down, agreed that their relationship mattered more than any differences that may have once existed, and committed themselves to the heavy lifting ahead. It is not easy to turn a cold peace into a warm one, perhaps even harder than to reconcile with those with whom sharp differences have kept us apart. But this I promise you, on none of our gravestones will it be written, "In the end ... he was right." It will or will not say: Beloved Father, Brother, Sister, Daughter, Mother. These are the things that truly matter, these are the "greater goods" of Yom Kippur. As Yehuda Amichai, the poet laureate of Israel, wrote in his poem "The Place We Are Right":

מן המקום שבו אנו צודקים	From the place where we are right
לא יצמחו לעולם	Flowers will never grow
פרחים באביב.	In the spring.
המקום שבו אנו צודקים	The place where we are right
הוא רמוס וקשה	Is hard and trampled
כמו חצר.	Like a yard.
אבל ספקות ואהבות עושים	But doubts and loves
את העולם לתחוח	Dig up the world
כמו הפרפרת, כמו חריש.	Like a mole, a plow.
ולחישה תשמע במקום	And a whisper will be heard in the place
שבו היה הבית	Where the ruined
אשר נחרב.	House once stood.

Self-certainty is not the soil out of which we grow, nor is it the means by which our relationships will be healed. Today, our pride softens and we widen our capacity for forgiveness. This is, after all, exactly what we ask of God – to abound in kindness and compassion, to not dwell on any single failure, to judge us based on the expansive arc of our lives, if not to include the lives of those who preceded us. The gates of repentance may appear as small as the eye of the needle but, in the divine mind, they can be made large enough for all the wagons and carriages of the penitent to pass through. So too, today, we must let through those people seeking reconciliation and return.

In the late summer of 1848, the Jewish community of Vilna was hit with a cholera epidemic of particular ferocity. Rabbi Yisroel Salanter, the rabbi of Vilna and dominant figure of nineteenth-century Orthodoxy, threw himself into the city's welfare, renting hospital quarters with five hundred beds, ordering his students to nurse the sick. The effects of the cholera were wrenching – unlike anything anyone had ever known – thirst, dehydration, intense pain in the limbs and stomach. Reb Yisroel, known for his punctilious observance of the law, feared that the upcoming fast of Yom Kippur would further weaken people and make them susceptible to the fatal disease. In the weeks preceding the fast day, he went so far as to hang placards throughout Vilna urging all those who felt weak to eat on the fast day to stave off the threat. Kol Nidre arrived, then the evening prayers and the morning prayers of Yom Kippur day, and Reb Yisroel saw that his pleas on behalf of public health were not being heeded by his weakened community. It was at this point, according to the accounts, at the conclusion of *shaḥarit*, in front of his entire community, that he did the most radical act of all, he rose to the *bimah*, publicly made *Kiddush*, drank and ate, so as to encourage all those in need to follow suit. It was a move not without controversy; following the holiday he was summoned before the rabbinical court of Vilna. But Reb Yisroel's knowledge and piety were beyond reproach. He defended his actions: "I am not lenient in regard to Yom Kippur; rather I am stringent when it comes to the laws of preservation of life." Reb Yisroel understood full well that there are times when one principle collides against another, and knew that his leadership would be defined by making a difficult choice in hopes of serving what he understood to be the needs of the hour.

Thank God, we are not living in a time of cholera and I have no plans to eat or drink. But we are living through a time of great challenge, with a cultural epidemic eating away at us all. Not just rabbis, but each and every one of us, has the means to address the pathology of the hour; we must draw on the quiet heroism within us all to contribute towards this healing, this *tikkun*, of our fractured world. If we can muster the courage to love each other as much as we love ourselves, if we can allow for the stakes to be higher than our own self interest, and if we can approach the relationships dearest to us with humility and a deep desire for reconciliation – we can, each one of us and all of us together, mend this world, mend our families, and mend our very souls that are desperately seeking repair.

"The Uprooted"

efore Oscar Handlin, there was one dominant narrative of American self-understanding – the frontier experience. From the Colonial "errand into the wilderness" to Daniel Boone's trip west, to Lewis and Clark's explorations, to Huck and Jim on the Mississippi, to Jack Kerouac's *On the Road*, to Springsteen's "Born to Run," our national story had been about an epic journey. All that changed in 1951, when Oscar Handlin wrote a book that forever revised how Americans see themselves. He didn't mean to. The Pulitzer Prize-winning book was meant to be a quiet study about immigration, entitled, *The Uprooted: The Epic Story of the Great Migrations that Made the American People.* In the first sentence of the book Handlin explains: "Once I thought to write a history of the immigrants in America. Then I discovered that the immigrants *were* American history." *The Uprooted* argues that far from being at the margins of the American story, the immigrant experience – specifically of the tens of millions of immigrants who poured into America between 1820 and World War I – *was* the American story. Handlin, who died this past month at the age of 95, had an impact far beyond the ivory tower of academia. His testimony before Congress on immigration law, quotas, and discrimination of all kinds played an important role in a national conversation that is only taking on increased importance day after day.

This morning, on this festival of Sukkot, I want to focus on one dimension of Handlin's book – not so much the impact that immigrants had or have on America, but rather the effect that the experience of emigration has on the immigrants themselves. There is something autobiographical about Handlin's research; he was himself the son of Russian

Jewish immigrant shopkeepers. In an almost lyrical style, Handlin tries to capture the voice and experience of people undergoing the process of uprooting. He explains the series of dislocations that occurred as immigrants went from a peasant European society, via a harsh and brutal crossing, into their port of arrival. Some are obvious: families were split apart, modes of labor shifted from agrarian to urban economies, and, of course, there were the complications that came with changes in language, culture, and the like. Handlin's most interesting observations describe more subtle but more profound changes, from the shift in gender roles as women entered the workforce to dramatic reversals in intergenerational relationships. In the Old World, wisdom and authority was based on the experience of the prior generation. But when an immigrant sends a child to public school, the direction of learning and authority reverses as the children are acclimated at a faster pace than the parents. Not all of the "uprootings" were negative. Handlin explains it was precisely because immigrants lacked any natural entrée into established professions that they often distinguished themselves in the arts, on the baseball diamond, or in other meritocratic pursuits. Handlin also points out that because immigrants were so uprooted from the structures of the Old World, they established a tight-knit sense of peoplehood and faith in America. In the shocks and aftershocks of alienation, one's church and ethnicity became a critical stabilizing element for each immigrant and every immigrant community.

This festival of Sukkot is the Jewish festival of uprooting, a study of our people's first and most formative national migration and all migrations since. Reflect on what it must have been like for 600,000 male Israelites, over two million souls, to leave hundreds of years of servitude in Egypt and travel though the wilderness for forty years towards the Promised Land. In many respects, I think the experience of ancient Israel fits Handlin's template quite neatly. First and foremost, we know that the sum effect of the forty years of wandering transformed the Israelites from a people longing for Egypt to a nation eagerly anticipating their arrival in the Promised Land. It wasn't easy. The desert generation died out, uprooted from the world they knew, unable to make the shift into their new setting. Even Moses himself was deemed by God unfit to lead the Israelites beyond the Jordan.

The second dimension of ancient Israel's uprooting was both necessary and ultimately, though not immediately, positive. They had to uproot themselves from being dependent on Pharaoh and Egyptian society and become dependent on God and themselves. As slaves under Pharaoh, the ancient Israelites had no notion of self-sufficiency. The manna, the miracles, the hunger, the trials of the desert, all were meant to teach Israel two critical traits that they lacked in the old world and would need in the new: "In order to teach you that man does not live on bread alone, but that man may live on anything that the Lord decrees." (Deut 8:3) The *sukkah*, both in ancient times and today, provides a corrective to the tendency to be excessively attached to turf, to rely on the idolatry wrought by materialism. A *sukkah* is an opportunity for every Israelite to remember that we stand subject not to the pyramids of Pharaoh, but to the majesty of God's creation.

And finally, as in the American immigrant experience, being uprooted from Egypt went hand-in-hand with the formation of a national identity. Of course, Israel knew they were a people apart when they were slaves in Egypt. But in Egypt it was a social stigma, not a mark of distinction. Only in the desert did being an Israelite mean standing in a covenantal relationship with God. Only in the desert did being an Israelite signal being party to a Promised Land and sacred destiny. Only in the desert did being an Israelite become something of which to be proud.

On Sukkot we are supposed to reflect on the effects of being uprooted. But the real question, the really interesting question for us, is not so much about American immigrants or Israelites of old but how this question applies to us, the present American Jewish community. American Jewry is far from monolithic but, at risk of making huge generalizations about an incredibly diverse landscape, let me suggest that our current condition reflects a unique blend of being both rooted and unrooted at the same time. Let me explain. We are rooted in the sense that unlike past generations we are totally at home in America. We are not fighting the establishment – we are the establishment. With our synagogues, summer camps, schools, and federations, our political, philanthropic, and social stature, American Jewry has made a footprint in America that far exceeds its nominal numbers. If you need proof of the rootedness of American Jewry, you need look no further than this beautiful synagogue to see evidence that we are here and here to stay.

But this is only half the story. While we are institutionally rooted, as individual Jews we are probably more "unrooted" than any other time. Take me for example. My parents are British, I was raised in Los Angeles, I went to school in Michigan and Chicago, and I live in New York and am married to a woman from Pittsburgh whom I met during a year living abroad. It is a fairly typical story. There is no reason to believe that, at 21, a Jew will be living in the same community as she did at age 13, or as she will at age 24; in fact, the odds are heavily against it. There are many reasons why the affiliation rates of Jews are so low, but I have to believe one of the most obvious reasons is that, through no fault of their own, a typical American Jew uproots himself or herself over and over again, in ways unimaginable to past generations. It is incredibly difficult to establish and re-establish one's roots, all the more so if you have no reason to believe that your present station in life is your final destination. If there ever was a holiday that reflected the challenges of being a contemporary American Jew, it is Sukkot. We live it not just this week, but every week of the year.

I think it is the responsibility of forward-looking Jewish institutions to embrace the *sukkah*-like reality of American Jewry. There should exist a coordinated network of Jewish life and living, whereby uprooted Jews can be identified and welcomed in by the very institutions that need their presence for their continued vitality. I am thinking of a global JDate or Jewish Facebook with a virtual profile of Jews wherever they are. For instance, when a child of Park Avenue Synagogue goes to college, the campus Hillel director should receive a call from me telling them that a terrific young adult is on his or her way, and we at Park Avenue will in turn be invested in the success of that Hillel. And on the other end, every Hillel or Birthright program should track their alumni into the Jewish community of their first graduate or professional position and should program accordingly. It is incumbent upon all of us to support a seamless transition from one chapter of Jewish existence to another. It would take a lot of money and a lot of staff hours. Most importantly, it would demand that all Jewish institutions, from synagogues to summer camps to Chabad houses to Birthright, recognize that it is not solely their own programs that are of paramount importance, but rather the soul of every Jew they claim to be serving. In a world of rooted institutions and unrooted Jews, we have to realize that the metric of success for any Jewish institution is that institution's ability, first, to cultivate a Jewish identity that can translate into a new context and, second, to warmly receive the products of other like-minded institutions.

In my own personal Jewish journey, Shabbat Ḥol HaMoed Sukkot holds a special place. It was on this Shabbat that I first walked into my campus Hillel my junior year of college – the beginning of a journey that continues to this day. It seems so silly in retrospect. I went to Jewish day school, my parents were leaders in their synagogue, we had Shabbat dinner every week, but I never entered college Hillel for the first two years of college. For all the seeds that were planted in me, what now seems painfully obvious was not so obvious way back then. Namely, that the most important feature of Jewish identity is its mobility, its ability to go with you wherever you go, a sense of peoplehood, of faith, of intellectual curiosity that – like a *sukkah* – moves with you at every stage of life.

From the experiences of ancient Israel, through every immigrant wandering, our strength is measured according to how our Jewishness withstands the uprooting process. The uprootings today are different than they have ever been, neither better nor worse, but uprootings every bit as momentous as those of former times. We ignore that fact at our own peril. This Sukkot, may we, yet another generation of wandering Jews, be attentive, vigilant, and creative in our response to the uprootings of the present generation so that we, like generations before, can arrive safely at our promised land.

"In the Garden and Beyond"

For reasons that are too strange to get into, I had the odd pleasure this past week of eating lunch with one of the nation's most prominent statisticians from the University of Chicago. Over the course of the meal, he shared with me the results of a study he conducted early in his career on risk management education for physicians. He researched what is the correlation, if any, between doctors taking risk management courses and malpractice claims. One would think, or at least I would, that there is a rather direct correlation. A physician who takes a risk management course would be much more cautious, perform much better, and hopefully have a far reduced incidence of malpractice claims.

The results of the study (which I have since read) argue otherwise. For most of the nearly 2000 participating doctors, not only did the number of malpractice claims not decrease after one or two risk management courses, but there was actually an *increase* in claim vulnerability. Short-term education, what you or I might call a "one-off," had the opposite effect than desired. The study went on to explain that the efficacy of risk management education only kicked in cumulatively, after additional, ongoing, and sustained investment and reinforcement by the physician. (Frisch, PR, et al. *West J Med*, Oct 1995, 163:4)

All in all, it was a good lunch, though the conversation did take me way out of my comfort zone. It made me think about what makes us tick, how we are wired as human beings, and what does and doesn't shape or change our behavior. I vividly recall when I took driver's education as a teenager in Southern California and we were all forced to watch a movie called *Red Asphalt*. The title says it all; it was basically a B-movie designed to scare the daylights out of soon-to-be drivers on the dangers of speeding, drinking, and other reckless teen behaviors. Yet, according to what my statistician friend was saying, this sort of "one-off" education may actually have little or even the opposite effect than desired. Lacking a sustained context, such tactics may throw the intended learner off balance, drawing one nearer to, not farther from, the unwanted behavior.

Every parent struggles with this question on some level. What is the best way to make sure your teen doesn't drink? To sit them down and give them a stern warning? Or is such a talk actually the quickest route towards your teenager being the first to taste the forbidden fruit? Alcohol, drugs, irresponsible sex – the question is the same. Big kids, big problems, little kids, little problems. This week, I sat down with my children to go over our household's Internet rules. How hard do I regulate? However much I trust my children, to not say something seems irresponsible. But how much do I say before my words have the opposite effect than that for which I am aiming?

There are no sure bets and I am figuring it out just like you are. I do take comfort in knowing that people a lot smarter than you or I have struggled with these same questions before. Not just people, but God. Long before Wendy Mogel, Jews already had a parenting book – the Torah. Think of the opening scenes of Genesis from which we read today. God is thrust into a parenting role with Adam and Eve in the Garden: "Of every tree of the garden you are free to eat; but as for the tree of knowledge … you must not eat of it, for as soon as you do, you shall die." (Gen 2:16–17) And sure enough, they do exactly what they are told not to do. The only surprising thing about how the story unfolds is that anyone, God included, is at all surprised by what happens. If, as Wallace Stevens has written, "not to have is the beginning of desire," then to tell someone they cannot have is the foundation stone for all transgressive behavior. The commandment was a "one-off," imposed from the outside. There was no follow up, not to mention the fact that it was actually untrue – they did not die when they ate the fruit. It was a clumsy concoction of counseled abstinence, prohibition, and lack of supervision or follow-up that resulted in humanity asserting itself against God's will. As is true for so many of us, God's first steps as a parent or manager backfired.

The good news is that God does improve – slowly. Just a chapter later, our attention turns to the children of Adam and Eve, and we encounter a downcast Cain. In this case, God does something very different than before. "You can do it, Cain," God says. "Sin may be crouching at your door and its urge may be towards you, but you can be its master." Unfortunately, Cain is not up to the test, but God's tactic has become less coercive and more supportive. God's follow-up question, "Where is your brother Abel?" does run contrary to all the parenting literature I have read in that it forces Cain into a posture of defensive lying, but overall there appears to be a learning curve. God seems to be self-correcting from past mistakes.

I think a wonderful way to read Genesis is as a story of God finding the right balance of laying down the law and understanding the limitations of such an approach. Humanity continues to fall short of expectations and God floods the earth; God chooses Noah to pick up the pieces. We build the tower of Babel and God knocks it down, never really explaining to humanity why building it was so wrong in the first place. It takes time, but eventually God realizes that relationships and moral character aren't built on "one-off" commands, lists of do's and don'ts, prohibitions and proscriptions.

Only with Abraham does God realize that the best way to get the desired results from humanity is actually by way of what the current literature on the subject will confirm: a statement of potential and promise. No threats, no huffing and puffing. "Your name shall be great, you will be a blessing." God will protect, God will be present. Abraham will have his good days and bad days, and so will God – but finally with Abraham one gets a sense that God is hitting the divine parenting stride. Only here does it seem that God learns that you can catch more flies with honey than with vinegar. Only here do we see that growth comes not from directives thrown down, but from humanity being endowed with a frame of reference by which to grow from within. It is not absolute; the children of Israel continue to act like children and they will experience both the divine carrot and the divine stick in the chapters ahead. But think of how far God and humanity have come from that first exchange in the Garden of Eden.

Everyone has his or her own theories about how to get people to change. The psychology of motivation is tremendously complex. Some people do it through a domineering and dictatorial style, scaring people into line. As Machiavelli counseled, if given the choice of being feared or loved, always choose fear. There are some, who like the late great owner of the Raiders, Al Davis, motivate by a "Just Win, Baby" philosophy. Some parents make life an incentive system of quid-pro-quo, a series of 'if-then' bribes. If you do your homework, then you will get TV time; if you do your job, then you will get a raise. Some people like to keep everyone off balance. I recently read an interview in the *The New York Times* with a business executive who, when an employee lost months of work and tons of data by forgetting to back up the hard drive, threw an ice cream party, figuring that more people will remember the misstep with a bellyful of ice cream than with a bellyful of yelling.

Probably the most Jewish tactic can be summed up in three Yiddish words: *es pasht nisht*. The expression can be translated as "it's not becoming," but when used on me, it always carried a sense of "we don't do that." As the psychologist Rabbi Abraham Twerski explained, better than berating, scaring, coercing, or coaxing someone towards a behavior that is ultimately not absorbed into one's sensibility, these three little Yiddish words assume a goodness within that ultimately can be referenced again and again as a rallying point for a person's self image.

There are all sorts of tactics, and I will be the first to admit that I have yet to crack the code. When it comes to getting a child to eat right or sleep through the night, every one of my kids responds differently, and in some battles I am still coming up empty.

But what I do know is that unlike other faith traditions, as Jews we believe that human behavior is neither predetermined nor best imposed from the outside with a one-off command. Who we are and who we seek to be ultimately comes from within. As the old psychology joke goes: How many psychologists does it take to change a light bulb? Only one, but the light bulb has to want to change. The Garden of Eden story is an example of what not to do, expecting a result merely by declaring a rule – lacking both context and follow-up. The corollaries are clear for all of us. Far too often, we walk around telling our kids to be safe, eat right, speak respectfully, take their Judaism seriously, as if simply saying the words will magically make it so. There are no guarantees in this world, and an awful lot just comes down to *mazel*. But next time you give advice, discipline, or caution, don't kid yourself into thinking that you can just say it and it will happen. "One-offs" didn't work for God, and there is no reason to believe they will work for you or me. Role modeling, reinforcement, providing a sustained context for whatever it is you are communicating, these are the things that will make a difference. Most of all remember that the source of all motivation, responsibility, and morality is not actually lodged in your words or in you for that matter, but that it is embedded in the heart and mind of the child with whom you are speaking. If nothing else, let them know they are bursting with potential, and make sure they know that you are there to support, correct, and steer their potential.

There are many important lessons to take from the Garden of Eden, but the most important one is this: the Garden of Eden doesn't last more than three chapters. For the next 184 chapters of the Torah, not to mention the rest of the Bible, humanity exists outside of the Garden. And the same is true for our children. Neither you nor I know just how long we will have our children in the Garden before they leave to make decisions of their own. What I do know, what weighs on me, is that the odds are that in the days and years ahead, when our children will make the momentous decisions affecting the direction of their lives, in all likelihood they will no longer be in our gardens for us to tell them what to do. Your best case, my best case, our best case scenario is that before that day we will have given them the tools to make the right choices, the self confidence to make decisions out of conviction and principle, and an abiding sense that though we may not be physically there at their side, our love, our presence, and our highest ideals are guiding them every step of the way.

Tol'dot
"Brother, Can You Spare a Blessing?"

To sit down at a large family Thanksgiving dinner is to experience the pleasures and pressures of family dynamics ... on steroids. All of our familial idiosyncrasies, fissures, and history are brought together around a single table for an exclusive one night engagement. Everyone's behavior becomes the subject of dissection and drama – a 24-hour news cycle before the era of cable news. Will the dinner-hosting daughter-in-law allow the well-meaning but sometimes boundary-breaking matriarch to bring her own dish to the dinner or not? Should a parent interfere in how a grandparent chooses to entertain, feed, or otherwise indulge their shared child/grandchild? Thousands of small decisions surrounding a single holiday meal touching on nerves whose sensitivities extend back decades if not generations.

Should you enjoy the blessing of sitting down at a dinner with extended family, you know the real intrigue is not so much across the generations, but within them – among siblings. Siblings are, as the saying goes, nature's way of creating slightly different versions of ourselves. A Thanksgiving dinner is like a house of mirrors as we look across at these alternative editions of who we are. We may no longer live in the same home and our lives have long since gone in different directions, but there is something about a brother or sister that burrows under your skin forever like no other relationship. To sit down for a meal and see the careers they have chosen, the spouses they keep, the decisions they are making for their children – it turns over the topsoil of your own identity in a way that nobody and nothing else can. By dint of our shared DNA and household of origin, they are probably the most honest and unforgiving prism by which to access our fears and hopes.

Siblings are our past, present and future all rolled up into one. Whenever I officiate at the funeral of someone who has achieved the blessing of length of years, it is the children and grandchildren who speak. The elderly brother or sister of the deceased usually sits quietly to the side like a footnote – Uncle So-and-So who flew in from out of town. But I have often thought that a slightly less gracious, but altogether more honest way to eulogize someone would be to have siblings do it. How was his life a reflection of the demons of his youth? How did her choice of spouse reflect a heartbreak that nobody in the room knows about – except a sister? In the timeline of our lives a sibling is our longest-standing relationship, and even after death can be a steady presence in our lives.

There is nothing like a brother to make you think deeply about your present. This past week, I listened to my brothers compare notes about the Little League teams they coach – how in addition to their busy careers and full lives, they swagger around soccer and baseball fields with their kids every weekend – more than once causing me spasms of inadequacy. Yet I know I am no saint when it comes to the competitive nature of fraternal relationships. When I joined a gym last year, the membership guy asked me what my goals were: aerobic fitness, muscle mass, maybe weight loss? I responded, "I have one and only one fitness goal: when I see my brothers, I want to be in better shape than they are." And then, of course, there is the role siblings will play in the years to come. The millions of decisions we make together about the relative who has yet to find his or her way, how parents will be cared for, or any of the other aspects of the shared language and responsibilities of siblings.

Jacob and Esau could not share a bowl of lentil soup without provocation, never mind a Thanksgiving dinner. Unlike modern psychology, the Torah does not find the primary shaper of human identity between parent and child, but rather between siblings. Beyond all the biblical fraternal dynamics we've read about so far – Cain and Abel, Isaac and Ishmael – it is the bond between Jacob and Esau that receives the fullest attention of our narrator. It is not clear, and I don't think it is meant to be, how much of their resentment is due to nature or nurture. Were the boys hardwired in their dispositions, or were their inclinations due to the clumsy parenting of Rebecca and Isaac? Esau, like Biff in *Death of a Salesman*, grew up on a steady diet of paternal praise, only to discover that the rest of the world operates on different principles. (See Jeffrey Kluger, *The Sibling Effect: What the Bonds Among Brothers and Sisters Reveal About Us*, p. 101) In Jacob's case, the blessings he received from the womb and onward come at the expense of having a functional relationship with anyone, ultimately forcing him to flee to create a family of his own. Divine oracle, birth order, genetics, parental favoritism – all contribute to a toxic concoction that pits them against each other from the moment of conception onward.

If I had to put my finger on the source of the problem, it would be the hazardous biblical belief that God's blessing is a zero-sum-game. Jacob and Esau believed that blessings and birthrights were by nature both limited in number and indivisible. Only one of the brothers could be a dweller of tents, only one of them a man of the field. Only one could be his father's favorite and only one his mother's. Only one could receive the birthright, only one could receive the sought-after blessing. Their competitive and destructive relationship was based on the corrosive idea that what one brother had, the other could not. They needed to box each other out for fear of becoming the brother left out. The most emotionally searing verse of the entire tale, if not the Torah itself, is Esau's cry to his father upon learning that Jacob had taken away his blessing. "Have you but one blessing, Father? Bless me too, Father." It was inconceivable to any of the family – Isaac, Rebecca, Esau, Jacob – or even God, that maybe, just maybe, life, love, and blessing need not be limited to only one of them. Nowhere does the biblical text allow for the possibility that when it comes to the things in life that really matter, the calculus of family dynamics could occur in an altogether different, more generous way.

While the biblical laws of primogeniture have long since fallen to wayside, I think deep down many of us somehow still believe, as Jacob and Esau did, that siblings operate in a zero-sum matrix. For some reason we let ourselves believe that there actually exists a wise child and a wicked child, an academic one and an athletic one. Against all logic and medical evidence, we think DNA is distributed first come, first served, like a black Friday sale – "get the musical gene now, quickly, before the second child arrives!" Or, if you like, that our family roles are auditioned off like parts in a musical, and only one person gets to play the lead. Because we see our own families, or even worse, our own children through this imagined, self-imposed lens, we emerge with what is ultimately a self-destructive way of looking at the world. After all, if there is a limit to God's blessing, then it is understandable that we should trip over the logical corollary – that our siblings' blessings come at the expense of our own.

Our biblical stories contain an unavoidable thread of destiny foretold. It would misrepresent the text to say otherwise. But it is also true that our subsequent tradition is a fierce defender of the notion that each of us is the captain of our own fate. You may or may not be musical, happily married, or professionally satisfied. But I promise you that the shortcomings and blessings of your life have absolutely nothing to do with the shortcomings and blessings of your siblings. Happiness is not a bowl of lentil soup that if one brother takes a gulp, less is left for the other. Of course there are inequities when it comes to the genetic lottery, and all parents fumble with the question of how best to encourage a child towards personal strengths without pigeon-holing him or her prematurely. But at a certain point, regardless of our birth order, the hand we have been dealt, or the missteps our parents may have made along the way, we are who we are and who we will become owing to nothing but our own choices. It is so painful to bear witness to people assessing their own potential – realized or failed – by comparison with their siblings. There should be only one answer to Esau's throbbing question. "Yes, of course there is more than one blessing." Life is not a football game where only one Harbaugh brother gets to win. The blessings that we seek are not commodities with set limits. The Midrash explains that the Messiah will not arrive until the tears of Esau cease to flow. In other words, only when siblings cease to experience Esau's agony – the mistaken belief that only one blessing exists – then and only then will redemption arrive.

Unfortunately, unhealthy sibling rivalries do not end with Jacob and Esau. They continue in the tale of Joseph and his brothers, the history of the Israelite monarchy and, for that matter, in the stories of our own families. We know the pitfalls even as we step in them. There is, thankfully, a glimmer of hope. Two weeks from now, Esau and Jacob will meet again after having spent decades apart. They will embrace and they will weep, putting the missteps of their past behind them. Jacob will come bearing gifts, and in response Esau will look at his brother and say, "I have enough," going on to state, "for to see your face, is to see the face of God." It is a profound and moving exchange that the sensitive reader understands to signal tremendous personal growth and a lesson for us all. "You, the measuring stick by which I assessed my own self-worth. You, whose countenance in our youth was a trigger for my own rage and a prod for my resentments. You, with whom I had so much in common but with whom I never shared. You are not my enemy, you are my brother, both of us created equally in the image of God, and now, years later, I know that there is more than enough to go around, there is more than enough blessing to share."

Israel Zangwill once wrote, "It takes two men to make one brother." As our biblical forebears learned, in order to be the brothers and sisters we want to be, we must first be sure that we are able to be the men and women we know that we can be, and to be grateful for what I believe to be the greatest gift of all: the gift of a sibling. This Thanksgiving weekend and in the years ahead, we should merit reciting at our tables the greatest and truest expression of thanks Jews know: "How good and how pleasant it is when siblings dwell together" (Psalms 133:1).

Coming Down the Mountain

When we read the story of the *Akedah*, the binding of Isaac, it is only natural for our attention to focus on certain well-trodden scenes. God commanding Abraham to take his son, his only son, the one he loves – Isaac – to the top of Har HaMoriah and sacrifice him. Abraham dutifully obeying God only to have his hand stayed at the last minute by the intervention of an angel. Every year we return to the same questions: Why the test in the first place? Why did Abraham respond as he did? What was he thinking as he journeyed towards the mountain? Did Isaac understand what was taking place? Where was Sarah in all the drama? And while these questions and others stand, this year I find myself drawn to a less obvious place, the final scene – the descent after the drama – as Isaac and Abraham come down the mountain. "And Abraham returned to his servants, and they departed together for Beersheba; and Abraham stayed in Beersheba." (Gen. 22:19) What if anything remained of the relationship between father and son? My thoughts turn to Isaac himself. What effect did his near-death experience have on him? How did he make sense of the world as he came down from the mountain?

As I was reading commentaries on the *Akedah*, I was moved by the insights of Elie Wiesel. Listen to what he wrote about Isaac. Because for Wiesel, more interesting, more difficult and more long-lasting than what took place at the top of the mountain, was how that incident was going to be remembered after the fact; by how Isaac would understand the incident in retrospect:

> What did happen to Isaac after he left Mount Moriah? He became a poet – author of the *minha* service – and did not break with society. Nor did he rebel

against life. Logically, he should have aspired to wandering, to the pursuit of oblivion. Instead he settled on his land, never to leave it again, retaining his name. He married, had children, refusing to let fate turn him into a bitter man. He felt neither hatred nor anger toward his contemporaries who did not share his experience. On the contrary, he liked them and showed concern for their well-being. After Moriah, he devoted his life and right to immortality to the defense of his people. (*Messengers of God: Biblical Portraits and Legends*, p. 96)

Wiesel continues to explain that at the end of time, Isaac will be privileged with a special place in God's presence. He will be entitled to say anything he wishes about God. Ask anything of Him. Because he suffered? No. Wiesel explains, "Suffering, in Jewish tradition confers no privileges. It all depends on what one makes of that suffering. Isaac knew how to transform it into prayer and love rather than into rancor and malediction. This is what gives him rights and powers no other man possesses." (*Messengers*, p. 97)

In Isaac, Wiesel sees not merely Abraham's son, but his own challenge, the challenge of post-Holocaust Jewry. "Of all the Biblical tales," writes Wiesel, "the one about Isaac is perhaps the most timeless and most relevant to our generation. We have known Jews who, like Abraham, witnessed the death of their children; who, like Isaac, lived the *Akedah* in the flesh." (*Messengers*, p. 95) Wiesel, who spent part of his childhood in Auschwitz, felt a special kinship with Isaac because of what he went through. But for Wiesel it goes deeper. The *Akedah* is an archetype of vital importance in understanding the Holocaust, because for Wiesel it is Isaac who is the first survivor. For Wiesel, Isaac's achievements following the *Akedah* are altogether noteworthy because he was able to leverage his suffering not towards death but towards life.

My "aha" moment in understanding Wiesel came as I was reacquainted with a decades-old speech of his in a recent article by our own Menachem Rosensaft. ("Transferring Memory: The Task of Children and Grandchildren of Holocaust Survivors," *Midstream*, Spring 2011) In a 1984 speech at the First International Conference of Children of Holocaust Survivors, Elie Wiesel addressed the challenges that came with growing up in the shadow of the Holocaust.

> The great majority of you [he explained] remain healthy and generous with a sense of humor, with a sense of literature and culture and humanity. That you are so well-adjusted seems almost abnormal. Logically, most of you should have ended up on the analyst's couch if not elsewhere. The fact is that you have managed to rechannel your sadness, your anger, your inherited memories into such humanistic endeavors as medicine, law, social action, education, philanthropy. In other words, you really are the worthy children of your parents. They have shown what they can do with their suffering; you are showing what you can do with your observation of their suffering ... In deciding to get married, to have children, to build on ruins, your parents sought to teach history a lesson: that we are not to give up on life, not to give in to despair...

Whether Wiesel's comments were meant to be descriptive or prescriptive, his remarks correctly identify the central challenge of living in the shadow of the Holocaust. Given the trauma, given the pain, given the covenantal obligation to remember and never forget, how exactly does one move forward? For Wiesel it is not an either/or proposition. Memory and the construction of identity go hand-in-hand. For those living in the wake of the Shoah, it is the ability to both remember and move forward in strength that marks the tension of what it is to be a Jew in a post-Holocaust world.

The Hasidic master Rabbi Menachem Mendel of Kotsk, when asked to identify the most difficult part of the Binding of Isaac, answered, "coming down the mountain." I think what he meant is that however anxiety-ridden the walk up the mountain may have been, however traumatic the incident at the top of the mountain, coming down the mountain bore a unique challenge, because only here were the participants able to make a choice on how to chart out the future. The choice of how to remember, the choice of how to live. Many believe that the *Akedah* rendered Isaac emotionally scarred and therefore unremarkable when compared to Abraham or Jacob – acted upon, never acting. I find myself drawn to Wiesel's interpretation, understanding in Isaac's descent from the mountain a degree of heroism unique to him. In Wiesel's words:

... Isaac remained a believer. ... Isaac, Yitzhak in Hebrew, means "he will laugh." So I asked myself, "How will he laugh?" and that is where I make the leap: Isaac, the first survivor of tragedy, of a holocaust, will teach us how to laugh, how to survive and how to go on believing. ("The First Survivor," Statement for the Niles Township Jewish Congregation, Skokie, Illinois, December 7, 1980)

In his most recent novel, *A Sense of an Ending*, Julian Barnes writes, "History isn't the lies of the victors ... It's more the memories of the survivors." As important as the events of our lives may be, perhaps more important is how we choose to remember those events. As Barnes writes elsewhere, "What you end up remembering isn't always the same as what you have witnessed." It is a fascinating thought, that our subjective and selective recollections ultimately dominate the objective history of who we are and how we came to be and ultimately, who we become.

There are those who focus on the climb up, there are those who focus on what happens at the top. These people are not wrong, but when it comes to who we are, what Isaac knew, what Wiesel knows, is that identity is shaped on the way down. Emerson once wrote that an institution is the lengthened shadow of one man. As a people, we know that our Judaism exists in the lengthened shadow of one mountain – Mount Moriah. The shadow is there. We cannot dodge it and it cannot be avoided. How we walk, how we respond, that is what determines who we are, today, tomorrow – every step of the way.

Va-yetzei
"The House of Laban"

From a historical perspective, there is nothing terribly surprising about the ethical failings we read about every day in the paper. Insider trading, phone hacking, influence peddling, steroids in sports, high school cheating scandals. We are momentarily aghast when we first hear these stories, but then, into the vacuum of our disbelief, come rushing in memories of other incidents of cheating, lying, adultery, and the like – all of which happened long before the present news cycle. Technology has endowed us with new ways to sin, and the Internet has emerged as a court of public opinion inconceivable to earlier generations. But the realization that human beings are subject to ethical failing – as Ecclesiastes wrote, "There is nothing new under the sun."

Ethical failing, depressing as it is, does not surprise me. What is jarring and what does still surprise me, is not the wrong that people do, but their insistence on transforming their "wrongs" into "rights," or at least "less wrong" wrongs, the *chutzpadik* human proclivity to contextualize, reason, equivocate, and justify our failings when standing accused of wrongdoing. Three quick examples: This week we read the testimony of the British phone hackers who not only insisted their actions were justified owing to their circulation-obsessed bosses, but that they were actually serving the public interest. "Phone hacking is a perfectly acceptable tool, given the sacrifices we make, if all we're trying to do is get to the truth." Second, the statement from a spokesman for a certain presidential candidate who defended accusations of adultery leveled at his boss, saying, "This appears to be an accusation of private, alleged consensual conduct between adults – a subject matter which is not a proper subject of inquiry by the media or the public."

And closer to home, in response to the Long Island cheating scandal, one writer wondered aloud if the scandal is not a natural consequence of the "hysterical quest for perfect grades, the Tiger mother goal of getting your kid into Harvard or Yale only." These examples are from just the last three days. I am sure we could cite a million more if given the chance. But I would be remiss if I didn't mention this fall's most heinous human failing, already and forever a self-standing class on ethics: Penn State. The crime itself was followed by a systematic abdication of moral responsibility by a chain of people in positions of power. Action by any of them would have protected vulnerable children from continued predatory abuse. Each instance of looking the other way represents an effort to hit the ethical snooze button, to spin human behavior and deflect blame by claiming that whatever the failing was, it was either none of anyone's business, or didn't really hurt anyone, or was what everyone else was doing, or was the unavoidable byproduct of a much graver societal evil that is actually far more deserving of our indignation. Who are we, these people would counter, to point fingers? Is there really such a sharp line between good and evil? Besides, were we to be in their shoes, facing their pressures – who is to say that we wouldn't have acted exactly the same way?!

Which is why, when it comes to Jewish ethics, the situation is sliced very, very differently. As far back as the Garden of Eden, good and evil never functioned on a sliding scale. There was and is good, and there was and is evil. We can tell the difference between the two. The medieval sage Maimonides explains that there is actually only one characteristic that differentiates human beings from every other living being: the ability to distinguish between good and evil and to do that which one pleases with absolutely no restraint. For purposes of today's discussion, that means that adultery is adultery, theft is theft, cheating is cheating, and no amount of mental gymnastics can blur those categories. And Judaism goes one step further. Not only does there exist absolute right and wrong, and not only do we have the ability to distinguish between the two, but we also readily acknowledge our urge and inclination to do wrong. Embedded within each of us is a *yetzer ha-tov* and a *yetzer ha-ra*, a good and an evil inclination. As my teacher Rabbi Louis Jacobs wrote, "The difference between Christianity and Judaism is that Christianity teaches that man sins because he is a sinner, while Judaism teaches that man is a sinner because he sins." (*A Jewish Theology*, 246) As Jews we believe that we have the most important thing of all, free choice. Which means that when we discuss ethics, the question is not whether or not there are really such categories as right and wrong. There are. The question is not whether or not we are capable of distinguishing between the two and making a free choice. We are. The question is whether or not we muster the combination of self-discipline and fear of heaven to actually do what we know we should do! It is never – *ever* – a defensible option to excuse our sins with the suggestion that it was our ignorance, our hardwiring, or our environment that is actually to blame.

A case in point is the central character of our *parashah* this week – Jacob. If there is one biblical figure who reminds us of the jagged moral nature of humanity, it is Jacob. Growing up in his parents' home, Jacob is manipulative, conniving, and exploitative, using every angle he can towards his personal advantage. But in this week's narrative, Jacob meets his match and then some. He enters the House of Laban, a twenty-year layover that our commentary calls a "dark night of the soul." Jacob is duped into marrying the wrong sister and subjected to his father-in-law's deceitful business practices. Laban's character is so treacherous that in the Passover *Haggadah* it is Laban's ill will towards our father Jacob that comes to embody all Jewish persecution. And yet – and this is the heart of the matter – in all of his flawed humanity Jacob holds his moral ground. He builds a business, he builds a family, and though he is given every reason to slouch towards the behavior of Laban's house, he chooses not to. Eventually Jacob is forced to set out on his own. He is pursued by Laban who levels stinging accusations against his son-in-law, accusations to which Jacobs responds, "For twenty years, I worked for you, never once partaking of your flock, making good on every loss..." Jacob forcefully insists that despite his surroundings, despite his own inner demons, he resisted the urge to do wrong. Jacob is a hero not because he is perfect. Jacob is many things, but he is no Abraham. Rather it is owing to the combination of self-discipline and fear of God – what he calls *paḥad Yitzhak*, the "fear of Isaac" – that he emerged unscathed and unblemished from Laban's house. The commentator Rashi explained that Jacob is called *shalem*, "whole" or "having integrity," because in spite of his environment, in spite of his inclination to do otherwise, how he should have behaved and how he actually behaved were one and the same. When called on the carpet by his accusers, Jacob in his righteous indignation was able to withstand the test.

Abraham, Isaac, Jacob, Joseph, Moses – what do all our biblical heroes have in common? At some point in their lives each one of them lived in a land of unsteady morality, a condition and state of affairs that makes them not too dissimilar from us. Jacob was not, to use Niebuhr's language, "a moral man in an immoral society," he was a man of mixed morality in an immoral society, and that is exactly the point. Jacob's stay in the House of Laban is given philosophical expression in Maimonides' introduction to the Ethics of our Fathers *(Shemoneh Perakim)*. Maimonides raises the fascinating and famous question as to who is more praiseworthy – the saint or the person who subdues his passions and exercises self-restraint? At home in the Aristotelian traditions of his day, Maimonides acknowledges that philosophers believe that it is the person who has no urge to do evil, who somehow transcends the desire to do wrong, who is saintly, and who has achieved the highest rung of moral character. Maimonides offers a different, more realistic way of looking at things. He explains that, according to the Rabbis, the person who desires and craves iniquity but does not do it is actually more praiseworthy than the person who feels no torment at refraining from evil. As the Talmud explains, "a person should not say 'I do not want to commit X, Y and Z sin.' Rather he should say, 'I do indeed want to sin, yet I must not, for my Father in heaven has forbidden it." As Ben Zoma taught in *Pirkei Avot*, "Who is mighty? The one who subdues his own passions." Or, if you like, as my granny of blessed memory told me, "Elliot, you can get your appetite anywhere you want, just make sure you always eat at home." Jacob is a model for us, because he struggles with the inner passions and outer pressures that could lead him astray and yet he emerges victorious, his character whole and intact.

Jewish ethics can be distilled into one word: "Ought." Ethical behavior occurs when what "ought" to happen actually does happen, and unethical behavior is in the gaping chasm that exists between what we ought to have done and what we actually did. People can argue among themselves about what is right and what is wrong, good and evil, and the prickly gray area in between. But at the end of the day it comes down to the all important "ought," an "ought" that is both irrefutable and inescapable in the courtroom of our soul. What ought I do? What ought I have done? Go ahead, try it. Plug in any tough decision you have faced. You don't need a rabbi to figure it out. There is right and there is wrong and you chose one of them. Just don't do what seems to be in vogue to do. Don't delude yourself or the people around you into thinking that you were only doing what you had to do, what everyone else was doing, or what anyone would have done under those same circumstances. When it comes to ethics, excuses are the tools of the incompetent used to build bridges that lead to nowhere.

Emerson once reflected: "It is easy in the world to live after the world's opinions; it is easy in solitude to live after your own; but the great man is he who in the midst of the crowd keeps with perfect sweetness the independence of solitude." We, like our patriarch Jacob, live in a world of swirling morality, there are many doorways to the House of Laban. We can neither control nor predict how the missteps of our time will be judged. Yet our hopes are as audacious as they are modest: to emerge as Jacob did, with the ability to shout out in the quiet sweetness of our soul that despite it all we did what we ought to have done and we are *shalem*, intact in our integrity, clear in our conscience.

Va-yeishev
"Aba-gate"

T wo weeks have passed since a series of videos produced by the Israeli Ministry of Absorption caused American Jewry to collectively bristle at the suggestion that Jewish life in America is so thin that the children of Israeli ex-pats living in America will, if they stay in America, assimilate into the melting pot of American life. Each advertisement cleverly played on the much feared moment when *Aba* turns to "Daddy," *Motek* to "Honey," concluding with the ominous post-script, "They will remain Israeli, their children will not." The entire eruption, dubbed "Aba-gate" by David Hazony, brought down the wrath of the ADL, JFNA, and all the other American Jewish organizations presently inundating your inbox for end-of-year donations. How can Israelis have the *chutzpah* to cast aspersions on American Jewish life? How dare they tell us that we are any less than they when it comes to Judaism?

Two weeks have passed, and let me suggest that the anxiety set off by the videos was not terribly new, was blown out of proportion and, most significantly, was entirely misdirected.

Let me explain.

For as long back as this week's *parashah*, Jews have felt the anxiety of what it means to leave *Eretz Yisrael*. Joseph's descent into Egypt marks a new stage in the formation of Jewish identity. Joseph did not have Internet access in Egypt, but if he had, then those ads would have been directed at him. With every departure of an Israelite from the Land of Israel – Joseph, Jacob, each of the brothers – the Torah is well aware of the fear that outside the Land, the connective tissue of our identity may fray, a fear that continues to this day. It may have lacked a certain sensitivity for Israelis to point out the tug of assimilation in

America, but such a claim is neither new nor necessarily wrong. Furthermore, the claim that Jewish life has the potential to hold a special texture in a Jewish state is a statement so obvious it borders on the banal. In fact, there is a word for it: Zionism.

All of us know, and if we don't, we should, that it is a challenge to raise children and grandchildren in the Diaspora with a strong Jewish identity. As is often the case with criticism, the only difference between what the ads claimed and what we ourselves already knew to be the case was the source of the comment. Besides, as Hazony wrote, since when have American Jews been shy about telling Israelis how to run their lives?! If a painful truth needs to be told about Jewish life in the Diaspora, then better it should come from within the family.

The most interesting aspect of "Aba-gate" is not what it said about American Jews; on that front the incident is neither new nor interesting. The most interesting thing about the ads, that almost everyone missed, was what they said about Jewish life in Israel. If anyone should reflect on the deeper import of these ads, it is Israelis. Because if you stop to consider the implicit message contained in the ads, then you know they express the inner Israeli anxiety that their identities are so thin – all nationalism and no Judaism – that once they leave the country, there is not enough Jewish substance left to survive an extended stay out of the homeland. It is hard enough to be Jewish in the Diaspora, but these ads make clear that typical secular Israelis lack the tools or inclination to associate with the Jewish community outside of the Land.

Permit me to paint a picture, and it is not a pretty one. Unlike here in America, Judaism in Israel, for better but often for worse, is controlled by the state. Marriage, divorce, burial, conversion – everything reflects, conforms to, and receives funding from the chief rabbinate, a chief rabbinate that does not recognize alternative expressions of Jewish life in Israel or, for that matter, in America. As liberal Jews we should be highly sensitive to the bitter irony that the modern state of Israel is a place where a Jew can be denied rights – as a Jew. In such a coercive and monopolized scenario, it is no surprise that many citizens have turned away from Judaism altogether. To use one such example, my own in-laws whom I will be visiting this week in Israel would never ever walk into a synagogue. They are Israelis through and through, but their inchoate Judaism has nothing to do with their national identity. This means that when they arrive outside of Israel – which for a variety and increasing number of reasons many Israelis do – they may speak Hebrew, but they have no inclination to connect to Jewish life.

And that is where the impetus comes for the ad campaign. The Israeli authors of these ads do not even reach for the word "Jewish." Israeli and Jewish are treated as two distinct concepts. As the head of our movement, Rabbi Julie Schonfeld, wrote this past week, "The ads make painfully clear the extent to which the concept of a meaningful Jewish identity in the Diaspora eludes Israelis." The ads challenge Israeli Jews to consider the host culture in which their Judaism takes shape: a struggle within Israeli, not American, Jewish life.

In just a few days we will gather in our homes around our menorahs to celebrate the miracle of Hanukkah. Hanukkah is about many things, including the miracle of the cruse of oil and the military victory over our oppressors. At its core, it describes a balancing act that continues right up to today: the ability to understand physical and spiritual strength not as an either/or proposition but as necessary and interdependent components of who we are. Hanukkah reminds us that Jewish sovereignty is important only insofar as it protects and encourages a vibrant Jewish life to emerge. The most important refrain of the Israeli national anthem Hatikvah is *Liḥiyot am ḥofshi b'artzeinu*, "To be a free nation in our land." These words are not only about the dream of a free Jewish state. They are about the dream that Israel aspire to be a place where all Jews are free to be the Jews they seek to be – Orthodox, Masorti, and Reform. A place where Jews of different stripes and types are able to exist side by side, proudly. A place for the free flourishing of Jewish identity, capable of withstanding the pressures of living in Israel, in America, or on the all important bridge between the two.

Va-y'ḥi

"It's Not Just a Bus, It's Israel"

If you have ever flown El Al to Israel, as I did last week and will do again this evening, then you are familiar with its marketing motto, "It's not just an airline, it's Israel." As the six Cosgroves piled into our seats, I reflected on the motto, "How very true – truer I bet than their marketing team intended." Right before my eyes, the lady in the row ahead of me removed my luggage from the overhead bin and placed it on the floor in the aisle. I watched incredulously, and asked her in Hebrew, "Excuse me, what do you think you are doing?!" She replied with unflinching moral clarity, "Well, I need a place for my bag." And yet, 30,000 feet, six hours and many cranky kids later, an altogether different sense of family emerges. People are holding each other's children, playing Jewish geography, and schmoozing with each other in a way that would be inconceivable on any other airline. For better and for worse, an El Al flight to Israel does represent more than just an airline – it represents Israel, with all its quirks, its blessings, and its flaws.

Sometimes an airline is not just an airline, and from the news coming out of Israel daily, sometimes a bus is not just a bus. Over fifty years after Rosa Parks, Ashdod resident Tania Rosenblit set off a national debate on gender-segregated public transportation when she refused to sit at the back of the bus despite the demands of ultra-Orthodox passengers. And while she continues to receive death threats, last week an IDF soldier, Doron Matalon, faced abusive sexual harassment when she similarly refused to move to the back of a Jerusalem bus. As we know from our own American history, in these cases the bus is not just a bus, but an insight into Israel, its quirks, its blessings, and its deeply troubling flaws.

Israel is one country that does not lack for problems. Iran, Gaza, the West Bank, the elections in Egypt, and the altogether troubling rise of the Muslim Brotherhood. There are massive and rapid shifts taking place when it comes to Israel's external existential security in response to which I believe we must all, as American Jews, be vigilant and active advocates. At the same time, I am hard pressed to think of a time when I can list so many internal existential concerns affecting the future health of the Jewish state. The bus segregation issue is but one of many. Last week, Rabbi Moshe Ravad, the Chief Rabbi of the Israeli Air Force, resigned, partially owing to new IDF instructions that religious cadets must attend ceremonies that feature women singing, which is prohibited according to the ultra-Orthodox community. Earlier in December, a group of right-wing activists attacked IDF soldiers in the West Bank, a shocking instance of Jew turning against Jew. Probably most public was last week's eruption in Beit Shemesh, when 10,000 people demonstrated in response to news of an eight-year-old Orthodox girl being spat on and verbally abused by Haredi Jews for walking to school in clothing deemed insufficiently "modest." This was followed by a despicable counter-protest, in which a group of over 1000 ultra-Orthodox gathered dressed in yellow stars and striped pajamas (images intended to evoke the concentration camps) and equating the Israeli response to religious intimidation with the actions of the Nazis.

The list goes on and on, from the seemingly small – a debate over whether a woman may eulogize a loved one at a funeral, or a religious man being asked to take off his *kippah* before entering a Tel-Aviv Internet café – to abhorrent acts of violence. These incidents, which have all occurred over the past month, are remarkable because they are happening within Israel, between Jews, and are all about the existential internal, not external, threats Israel faces.

You, like me, have watched these incidents and the reactions of the Jewish world, and have heard the range of outrage and indignation at the misogyny, the ignorance, and the medievalism of the ultra-Orthodox. It is tempting, especially as a non-Orthodox Diaspora rabbi, to weigh in with my own sensibility and to wish that Israel could somehow be recast as the Upper East Side. It is all too easy to project onto others our fears of an obscurantist orthodoxy, to make the Haredim the Jews we love to hate. But we must, as our tradition teaches, be *metu-*

nim ba-din, careful in our judgment, wary of efforts to classify the entire world according to our own categories. It is as myopic and misdirected to wish for the Judaism of Beit Shemesh to look like ours as the other way around.

We should also be careful not – as I have done for rhetorical effect – to throw all these incidents together, as if they are all the same. It is tempting, dangerously so, to try to conjure up some grand theory on what this all means and why it is happening. But there is a difference between an IDF officer standing up for a religious principle, whether it is to have a kosher meal or to not be asked to listen to a woman's singing voice – both equally valid Jewish legal categories – and a Jewish terrorist attacking the very army defending the Jewish nation. There is a difference between a community internally and collectively creating a standard of observance and that same community insisting that their practice hold sway for everyone else. Each incident must be understood on its own terms and we must caution against efforts to impose an ill-fitting monolithic explanation.

Finally, we need to be absolutely unyielding in calling out barbaric behavior when we see it. Spitting on someone is spitting on someone, whether the spitter is in a Hasidic *shtreimel* with long *payos* or not; thuggishness is thuggishness no matter who you are. Violence against an IDF soldier is terrorism, whether performed by a Palestinian or a West Bank settler, and wearing a yellow star on your arm to draw an equivalence between your own condition and the six million men, women, and children murdered in the Shoah, is a desecration of the highest degree, no matter what your cause is. For all our efforts to understand the other – and believe me, I give my brothers and sisters far more rope than most, more than I myself sometimes think they deserve – we cannot and should not stop expressing our outrage. Don't forget that when Jacob blesses his twelve children in this week's *parashah*, the first three children are redressed as much as they are blessed. Neither a father's love nor a brother's loyalty asks us to overlook outrageous and terrible things. Being Jewish, or Israeli, or religious does not grant you a free pass, even and especially not from members of your own Jewish family.

The challenge Israel faces is not so different from the challenge that Jacob understood as he blessed his children in this morning's Torah reading. How do you create a collective and united sense of what it is to be a child of Israel, brothers to each other, and at the same time acknowledge that each sibling, each tribe, is wired differently and aspires to different things. "Come together that I may tell you," Jacob says to the twelve children at his deathbed. Then he proceeds to give each child a blessing, and at the end, the text concludes, "And this is what their father said to them, each one their blessing." The medieval commentator Saadia Gaon picks up on the poetry of the verse, expanding it to "Each one, according to the blessing appropriate to him." Like the words of Torah at Mount Sinai, Jacob's final testament to his children, though it came from a single source, was received according to the capacity of each listener. It required them to recognize their shared ancestry and destiny, their common fraternity, and their differences at one and the same time. It is an incredibly difficult message to communicate and infinitely more difficult to absorb and to actualize, but Jacob knew that the future health of Israel would be found in the brothers' ability to see themselves as individuals all the while respecting each other and working towards a greater unity.

This is exactly the challenge that Israel faces today. The state of Israel is the grandest experiment of all – realizing the dream of creating a Jewish nation capable of housing multiple expressions of Judaism and yet, in the words of the Prime Minister this past week, also "a Western liberal democracy." Neither a theocracy nor a wholly secular state, Israel has a responsibility to allow for freedom of Jewish expression – liberal, Haredi, or none at all – and to see to it that these multiple and competing expressions are able to exist side-by-side in supporting a common nation.

The fulfillment of this dream would be difficult enough on a good day. It is made all the more difficult due to a toxic political and religious system that enables particular tribes, at one and the same time, both to separate themselves from the Zionist whole *and* to exercise a coercive and thuggish sway over others. As I mentioned a few weeks ago, it is not surprising that in such an environment, secular Israelis have found themselves being distanced from the Jewishness of the Jewish state. I recently read that the well-known Israeli novelist Yoran Kaniuk successfully petitioned the Israeli Interior Ministry to change his religion status from "Jewish" to "no religion." Kaniuk's petition was approved and he is now considered a Jew by nationality, but not by religion.

Others are following his move, even giving rise to a new verb, *l'hitka-niuk*, "to Kaniuk oneself," that is, to separate oneself from the Jewish religion. The non-religious are becoming anti-religious; the non-Zionist, anti-Zionist, and whether it is coming from faith or from fear, the modern day tribes of Israeli society are failing to sit down at a table to call each other brothers and sisters, children of the same Israel.

The future does not bode well. If present trends continue, there will be a demographic/democratic point of no return. Some people think we have already passed it. Being wired the way I am, I would rather think we need to recognize this moment for what it is: a Ben Gurion moment of big decisions and bold compromises that asks all of Israel to address the domestic, social, political, educational, and religious issues that are being exacerbated with each passing day. The goal is not to create a secular state; the goal is not to create a theocracy. The goal is to create a place where, in the words of the prophet Micah, "Each person will sit under their own vine knowing no fear." Our plucky little "start-up" nation needs to turn all that ingenuity onto itself and take the bold steps that will enable us to continue to be a light unto nations.

When we landed in Israel this past week, as many of you may have experienced, a particularly grating version of *"Heiveinu Shalom Alei-chem"* began to play through the loudspeakers of the airplane. My daughter turned to me and complained, "Daddy, why are they playing this song, it's so annoying, can't someone turn it off?" I responded by asking, "How many Jewish countries are there in the world?"

"One."

"And is there any other country or airline in the world that plays *"Heiveinu Shalom Aleichem"* when you land?"

"No."

"So I'll tell you what we are going to do. We are all going to listen to this music until they let us off the plane and we are going to be grateful that we get to live in a time that Israel exists and however obnoxious the background noise is, we will be grateful that we get to listen to it."

And that is exactly what we did, and that is exactly what we, on this cramped and bumpy airplane ride of being proud Jews and proud Zionists, need to do. We are going to work out a way to sit on this plane together and support the efforts of those with the same goals. We are going to accept the fact that we don't always like the background music, but remember each and every day that for all our objections, we are privileged to live in the presence of the modern state of Israel. The goal is not to create a Jewish state that mirrors your precise sensibility. The goal is to create a place where brothers and sisters can sit and live and flourish side-by-side, in all their differences, enjoying the blessings and shared responsibility of what it means to be a child of Israel.

Sh'mot

"Humanity and Hope"

L ast Saturday night, like the spies sent by Moses, I boarded a plane to scout out the land of Israel. I have been to Israel more times than I can count and I have lived there on and off during my life. I have been there with our congregation three times in the past two years and I was actually there just two weeks ago to visit my in-laws. But this trip was a first. This trip, organized by my esteemed colleague Rabbi Ammiel Hirsch of Stephen Wise Free Synagogue, was an interfaith trip of senior religious leadership from New York congregations. Rabbis, ministers, and imams of different stripes were sent to see Israel and the Palestinian territories first hand, meet with senior leadership, model an example of interfaith cooperation for all to see, and return to New York energized to share our experiences with our own congregations and the wider New York community. We met with journalists, politicians and regular folk and with religious leaders in the Jewish, Christian and Muslim community. We met with Knesset members; we met with Natan Sharansky; we met with the Mayors of Bethlehem, Haifa, and Sderot. We met with Salam Fayyad, the Prime Minister of the Palestinian Authority. Best of all, we met with the President of Israel, Shimon Peres, which I have to say was just about the coolest thing I have ever done. To sit in dialogue with a living legend was high on my bucket list, and while I imagine meeting with me was not high on his list, that experience alone made the trip worthwhile.

So what did we discover? Are we returning with a good report or a bad report? While I cannot speak for my colleagues, for me the answer is a little of both. Over the course of the few days there were moments of deep hopelessness as we heard leaders who professed two

vastly different historical narratives, narratives that cannot be reconciled. We stood on an outlook on the border of Gaza and were instructed by our guide about where to go should we hear a siren
signaling an incoming rocket. We walked around the Kotel and onto
the Temple Mount, humbled not only by the palpable feeling of God's
nearness, but also by the overwhelming distance to cross to arrive at
a territorial compromise. We heard about the toxic politics of both
the Israelis and the Palestinians, and the present reality that precludes
the possibility of grand Begin or Sadat-like gestures towards peace.
There is a bitter irony that this place that gave birth to the aspirations
of so many in the past, has come to serve as the site of the stillborn
dreams of the present.

But we also saw hope. And while distant, we felt the possibility of
peace. Interestingly, we felt it most in places that are left off typical Israel trip itineraries. We visited the Rabin Medical Center in Petach
Tikvah – a first class hospital that is the envy of the international medical community. We met there with a Palestinian doctor from the West
Bank, a woman who treats Jew and Arab alike. We heard about her
relationships with the Gazan community and how patients are brought
into Israel for treatment. Think about that: a West Bank doctor, working in an Israeli hospital treating patients from Gaza.

We saw hope in Haifa at a cultural center called Beit Hagefen,
where Jews and Arabs, Christians and Muslims produce art, music, and
theatre together. We went to Jaffa and met with Jewish and Muslim
businessmen and women working together for profit and, by extension, for peace. I spoke to Rabbi Roberto Arbiv, a friend of our congregation, who runs a "Children of Abraham" study group bringing
together a rotation of teachers for learning and dialogue among the
three Abrahamic faiths. In each of these places, and there were others,
we could see the flicker of peace, the possibility of reconciliation.

If I had to posit a theory on the distinction between hope and
hopelessness, peace and strife, it boils down to one thing – human
contact. The places with the most promise were the places where Jews
and Arabs, no matter what their differences – political, territorial, religious, or otherwise – knew the other, and understood that the other
is a fellow human being. It was not that the residents of Jaffa or Haifa
or the hospitals are any closer to a solution to the conflict, but rather

that they have the same starting point – the common hope of a human being for self-determination, mutual recognition, and equality. The places that lacked hope were the places where there was no semblance of co-existence, no contact with the other, no recognition of the other's humanity. The space between the Mediterranean and the Jordan is tiny, smaller than New Jersey, but it is subdivided and balkanized like no other place in the world – increasingly so. When you don't have contact with the other, then you don't see the other as a human being, and then the odds of achieving understanding and peace drop precipitously.

Think about this week's Torah reading – it is a case study in the relationship between humanity and hope. The moments of hope occur when the primary figures recognize another's humanity; strife occurs when that humanity is overlooked. Why were the Israelites enslaved? Because a new king arose who did not know Joseph. In other words, the Israelites were enslaved when they became faceless ethnic interlopers. "Throw all the male Hebrew children into the Nile," orders Pharoah. And the first act of civil disobedience occurs when two midwives, Shifra and Puah – not Hebrews but Egyptians – see that these children ... are children, and they resist the inhumanity of Pharoah's decree. Surely Pharoah's daughter, of all people, knew of her father's command. She happens upon Moses in the very Nile in which Hebrew children were being drowned. But she saw what Pharoah did not or could not see ... a child; and it was there that redemption began. At the dramatic moment when Moses steps into his own, he sees an Egyptian man *(ish mitzri)* strike a Hebrew man *(ish ivri)*, and Moses looks hither and hither and sees that there was no man, *ish*. There is a poetry to the verse, as if it is saying that in the eyes of the Egyptian, the Hebrew man did not possess *enoshiyut*, human attributes. He was a faceless Hebrew and thus to strike him was no crime at all.

It is such an obvious insight into human nature, but one that can never be emphasized enough. The most consistent predictor of hatred of any kind is the degree to which we are sheltered from contact with those whom we have been raised to hate. Homophobia, racism, anti-Semitism, religious hatred of any kind, the roots of which are manifold, are given to fester in the air of ignorance. On this weekend especially, we are keenly aware of Martin Luther King Jr.'s comment:

Men often hate each other because they fear each other; they fear each other because they don't know each other; they don't know each other because they cannot communicate; they cannot communicate because they are separated. (*Stride Toward Freedom: The Montgomery Story*, 1958)

God's plan for a diverse humanity only comes by way of a first principle – that we all share a common humanity, created equally in the divine image. The leader of the Latin Patriarchate in Jerusalem's Old City shared with us the story of the tourist who went to heaven and was being shown around by St. Peter. They went from cloud to cloud arriving at various doors, which St. Peter would open. He opened one room to see a large group rolling on the floor and talking in tongues. "Our Pentecostals," St. Peter said. Next he opened the door to a room filled with men dancing the *hora*. "Our Jews," said St. Peter. At the next cloud, he didn't open the door but instead put his forefinger to his lips in the hush motion and they both tiptoed past. Once past, the tourist asked, "What was that was all about!?" "Those are the Catholics," St. Peter explained. "They think they are the only ones here." The priest's point was clear. It is a short and slippery path from segregating yourself from others to believing that the other is lesser in humanity than you.

My take-home message, the message I share with you and look to act on in the years ahead, is that if we truly love Israel, then we will work passionately towards Israeli-Arab co-existence. I don't know if there will ever be a day when the Palestinians and Israelis agree on the history of the region. I am skeptical that the governments will muster the political will to make peace. I see no easy solution to the territorial disputes and I certainly have my doubts as to whether religions are capable of turning on a dime. But I do think people are people. And I think that the only hope for the region is to plant more and more seeds of peace, points of contact between human beings, cultural, economic, educational, and otherwise. Peace will not arrive "top down," neither by way of divine intervention nor from governments. It will come from the ground up, from enough people on both sides saying, "Enough, I know the other, and though we may differ, they are people too and they have a right to exist." We are told that we can only express our support for Israel by being on the political right or left. That is a false choice. Whatever our political differences may be, we can support Israel by supporting co-existence. Walls are important for Israel's security, but so are bridges, bridges of understanding, bridges to peace. Our tradition teaches *Adonai oz l'amo yiten, Adonai y'varekh et amo va-shalom.* Just as God bestows strength and peace to Israel in a single verse, so we too must see strength and peace as values capable of being spoken and embraced at one and the same time.

In his must-read book, *The Prime Ministers,* Yehuda Avner tells the story of the months following the 1979 Peace Treaty between Israel and Egypt. Prime Minister Begin and President Sadat met in El Arish to begin the implementation of the Peace Treaty. At Begin's instigation and with Sadat's concurrence, they were accompanied by buses filled with disabled veterans of the two armies: soldiers maimed in the wars of 1948, '56, '67, '70 and '73. As the leaders left to go about their negotiations, the busloads emptied out into the meeting hall. First came about 70 Egyptians of various rank and insignia. Some in wheelchairs, their legs amputated; a number grotesquely disfigured; many entering with the assistance of medical orderlies. Then the Israelis arrived, likewise disfigured, some paralyzed, others blind, hobbling into the hall on the opposite side from the Egyptians.

In the silence, the eyes of the two sides locked in a palpable maelstorm of conflicting emotions. "Which one," writes Avner, "had pressed the trigger, pulled the pin, pushed the button?" Nobody it seemed, had thought through the next step, how exactly they were expected to cross the room, a distance of only a few yards, an impassable no-man's land. Some began to motion to leave the room.

It was precisely at that moment, Avner continues, that a blind Israeli bent over to his young son at his side and whispered to him, "*Kach oti eleihem* [take me to them]," to which the child responded pleadingly "*Ani m'fached mihem,* [I am scared of them.]" Gently the father nudged his child to lead him to the middle of the room; upon his very first step, an Egyptian officer in a wheelchair, legless, began to roll himself towards them. Meeting in the middle, the officer placed the blind man's palm into his own and shook it. A Jew began to clap, was joined by an Arab, the sprinkle of claps swelling into boisterous applause as the two groups moved towards each other into a huddle of embraces, handshakes and backslapping. It was at this point that the leaders of the two countries entered and the applause rose to an even higher pitch and the leaders circulated amongst the men, asked them where they had fought, many in the crowd weeping and calling to each other in Hebrew, Arabic, and English, *Lechayim, Lihayot, To Life.*

In the midst of it all, the child clung to his blind father, bewildered, looking at the animated faces of Arab and Jew. As long as he could remember, he had played escort to his father who would never see because he had been made blind by the Arabs. To him, they would always be the enemy and by definition, bad. Sensing his son's apprehension, the blind man lifted his child into his arms, kissed him gently and said. *"Al tefached b'ni. Ha'Aravim ha'eyle tovim.* [Don't be afraid my son. These Arabs are good.]" (Adapted from Y. Avner, *The Prime Ministers*)

There are those who believe that peace between Israelis and Palestinians is a dream that can never be reached, a fool's errand, a delusion in a region filled only with hatred. I think the delusional ones are not those seeking peace but the other way around. It is those who shoot rockets into Israel thinking that Israelis will pack up and leave who are not only delusional but undercutting their own people's dreams for sovereignty and self determination. It is those who build and build thinking that nobody recognizes that these actions are in direct conflict with Israel's stated policy of a two-state solution who are delusional. I may be a dreamer, but I would take my dreams over their delusions any day of the week, not just because I like my dreams more, but because I think they have more of a chance of becoming a reality. It won't happen overnight; it will take years and years of tireless effort towards co-existence. We can be part of that effort, encouraging and supporting those committed to doing the same; and we can, here in the New York community, serve as a model for others, through dialogue, through friendship, and through courageous acts of bridge building in this fractured world in such desperate need of repair.

Yitro
"Giving Room to Grow"

There is one family relationship so prickly that I can only discuss it openly while my wife and children are away spending the weekend with my father-in-law, namely, the relationship between a man ... and his father-in-law. That delicate and raw and charged relationship you have with the man who, prior to your arrival on the scene, was the primary male figure in the life of that woman who is now called your wife. For better or for worse, there is an inescapable and disorienting mirroring effect that man has on you, because in your wife's eyes, the standard he set is the default measure of your own personal, professional, and domestic worth. Spending time with kids (or not), washing the dishes (or not), professional expectations. Depending on you, depending on your father-in-law – most of all, depending on the woman that binds you – you may rank higher, you may rank lower, but make no mistake about it, ranked you are. It is a condition that, to the best of my knowledge, can be ameliorated only if and when you and your father-in-law are rendered irrelevant by the merciful arrival of a far superior male, a son born to your wife. To quote my wife, "Finally, a man in this universe who really understands me." Those father-in-law visits, those "check ins" on how work is going, how the kids are doing. Does he really care about me? Is he checking "in" or checking "up" – on me? Even if you have achieved some success in your life, even if you are successfully supporting his daughter and grandchildren, you are never totally secure. I remember what the Cardinal said to my father-in-law as they sat next to each other listening to me speak at my installation here at Park Avenue Synagogue. He whispered, "Behind every successful son-in-law is a shocked father-in-law." Which, when you stop to think about, is a really interesting thing to hear from the mouth of a Cardinal.

All this serves as background as to why this week's *parashah*, *Yitro*, is one of my favorites. With the Israelites' enslavement and the Exodus behind them, and Mount Sinai yet to happen, the Torah reading describes the arrival of Moses' father-in-law Yitro with his daughter, Moses' wife Zipporah, and the kids – Gershon and Eliezer. They embrace, they order in dinner (just like I do when my father-in-law visits) and Moses tells his father-in-law about the exciting deliverance from Egypt. Monday morning arrives, Moses heads into the office to sit as magistrate for all the people. He comes home late that night having left his wife, kids, and father-in-law together all day. He is tired, he is exhausted, he puts his bag down, and all of a sudden (and I suspect many of us have been in this exact position), the guy starts laying into him. "Why are you working so hard? You are wearing yourself thin! Is this what every Monday looks like?" Yitro is the one guy in the world who doesn't care who Moses is! Pharaoh, Shmaraoh! Yitro could care less about the parting of the sea. Yitro is a father and a grandfather, and Yitro has what to say about how his son-in-law runs his front office.

This year, I have a new, slightly more subtle take on Yitro's advice to Moses. Traditionally, Yitro's criticism of Moses is understood to be that Moses has too much on his plate. Moses needs to set up a judicial system because otherwise he will wear himself out. I always understood Yitro's advice to be coming from a place of concern for his daughter and his grandsons – that Moses should be doing homework with the kids, having a date night with Zipporah. This year I read the text a little more slowly to understand exactly what else was at issue. When asked why he does what he does, Moses responds to Yitro, "It is because the people come to me to inquire of God. When they have a dispute, it comes before me, and I decide between one person and another, and I make known the laws and teachings of God." (Ex 18:15–16) The response gives a fascinating and troubling insight into Moses' understanding of his role in the community. From his answer to his father-in-law, it would seem that Moses believes that he has the ability – like an oracle – to communicate the laws, will, and truth of God. Moses thinks that his job is to give people up/down answers so that they can function. Yitro hears his son-in-law and tells him outright, "It is not good what you are doing." Remember, Yitro has stature of his own. He is, after all, a priest of Midian, and he knows something that

Moses has yet to learn and needs to learn about leadership. When people come to you with a concern, dispute or question, it is not necessary, prudent, nor perhaps even desirable to respond by telling them what they should or shouldn't do. Whether or not Moses had a direct line to the heavens is beside the point. True leadership, as Yitro relays to Moses, lies in realizing that even when you know – or think you know – exactly what should happen, your role is actually to let the other person arrive at a decision, law, or conclusion on their own.

This week has been, hands down, one of the fullest weeks I can recall since I arrived as rabbi in this community. Thank God there have been many happy occasions, including our double *simcha* this morning. But if you have followed the community emails then you know that there have also been so many members of our community who have lost family members. And beyond the passings, there are countless happenings under the radar – marriages tearing apart at the seams, fractures emerging between generations in families, and far too many quiet heartaches. The most difficult part for me is not the volume, not the painful but unavoidable reality of death or loss. The difficult part is learning to practice what Yitro knew all along, that sometimes – even when you have an opinion, even when you have seen the exact circumstance before, even when you know exactly what Jewish law does or doesn't say – your role is not to force a person's hand, or even worse, to be perceived as having tried to force someone's hand towards making a decision not their own.

A quick example. On several occasions these past few weeks, I have sat with families as they have made difficult end-of-life decisions for loved ones. As you may know, Jewish law is actually rather clear in this area. If the possibility exists of recovery, you choose life. But if the interventional steps you may take are not about giving life, but rather prolonging the inevitable onset of death, then according to the tradition such an act is not considered "choosing life," and one is permitted if not obligated to let a loved one die in peace and dignity. While I can sit in a hospital room and tell that to a family, I learned this week that my role is not to tell them what to do, but rather to answer their questions and give them the tools to arrive at the decision that will ultimately be theirs with which to live. I could give a million examples: parents and children arguing over matters of either petty or great consequence; siblings negotiating how to mourn a parent; families caught between celebration and loss. No matter how varied the situations may be, they all share two elements. First, in every case, I definitely had an opinion of what I thought should happen. And second, I tried my best not to tell the person or family what to do. They may or may not have done what I thought they should do, but by providing guidance and setting out choices at critical moments and by insisting that grownups make their own decisions, I would like to think that, at the very least, people were able to arrive at and own the decisions that will be theirs to live with in the years to come.

Yitro knew, and Moses came to know, that as important as it is to provide a forceful leadership presence, so too is it important to believe in people's capacity for self assertion and the need for every person to cultivate confidence in making his or her choices. Telling someone what they should or shouldn't do or did or didn't do right has its place, don't get me wrong – I am a father of four; I do it all the time. But I also know that the whole point of parenting is to prepare my child for the day when he or she will have to make the right choices without me in the room. I have to believe that it is only by giving people the space to articulate their own voice in the safety of trusted loved ones around, that they will be able to do so with confidence later on. It should not be lost on us that at every major pivot point of moral development in the Bible, from Genesis to Jonah, God shapes human character not by way of do's and don'ts but rather through a series of well placed interrogatives. "Where are you?" God asks Adam as he hid in the Garden. "Where is your brother Abel?" God asks Cain as his brother lay slain on the ground. Did God not know what was going on? Did God not have an opinion on the matter? Of course God did. But God knew that moral development, character, and a sense of self were only going to happen if humanity was given a chance to respond to God and to arrive at their own stance.

One of the most provocative insights on our Torah reading today regarding the giving of the law at Mount Sinai is the suggestion that in actual fact only the first word, *anokhi*, "I am" was spoken by God at Mount Sinai. The rest – all the subsequent legislation, as Rosenzweig famously explained – was the human response to God's presence. If there was ever a "top down" moment of God's will being made known

– it was at Mount Sinai. But even here the rabbis bristled, for they knew that in order for Revelation to "stick" it would have to come upwards from the people themselves.

And if this is the case for God, that even God recognizes the need to withdraw presence in order for humanity to assert presence – then how much more so for us?! We all need to allow for the rather counterintuitive possibility that our best and most active influence may be by way of active, engaged, and empathetic listening. When dealing with the people we care for most, cautious and thoughtful and self-censoring counsel builds trust, empowers our loved ones – and in that inevitable moment when we do need our voice to be heard and heeded – increases the odds that the other person will believe what is actually the case, that what we are saying is in his or her best interests. We are too quick to impose our own judgments on others, transferring our own rights and wrongs to people who, at the end of the day, are not us and who will have to live with their decisions for a long time after we have left the scene. Far too often we instinctively barrel down the field like a running back into the end zone forgetting that the point is actually to down the ball at the goal line. It is a risky business, but sometimes in life the goal is not to score. Sometimes, the goal is to fall just a little short in order to nervously see what will happen on the next play.

The great 18th-century philosopher Lessing once wrote, "Not the truth which someone possesses or believes he possesses, but the honest effort he has made to get at the truth, constitutes a human being's worth." The most telling thing Yitro does in the entire *parashah* is neither his counseling, nor the establishment of a judiciary. His most instructive act is that he knows when it is time to leave, *Va-yelekh lo el artzo*, "And he went on his way to his land." Yitro gave his son-in-law the tools and advice, but he also knew that it was only through Moses' own efforts that Moses would find his self worth, that Moses would become his own man, that Moses would become Moses. So too, may each of us learn that our loved one's self worth comes only by way of their own efforts, and may we have the wisdom and self-discipline to withdraw just enough that others can grow into their own.

"It's Not Just a Menorah"

When it comes to an appreciation of culture, my tastes tend to be more "Big Ten" than "Ivy League." I will not knowingly go to a movie with subtitles. I like my food to come in a bun. I have never attended the opera without falling asleep, and only under pressure could I tell you the difference between Manet and Monet. In college, I did take an art history class once, literally, dropping it long before it would appear on my transcript. As for recognizing classical music, my range is limited to the melodies on my children's Baby Mozart DVDs.

So it came as an absolute surprise to me last week in Rome that I was deeply moved and emotionally taken when standing face-to-face with an ancient arch located halfway between the Roman Forum and the Coliseum. It wasn't just any arch, but the Arch of Titus, and my heart was pounding as I found myself looking at an image that I had only ever heard about: the frieze depicting the triumphal procession of Roman soldiers parading the spoils of Jerusalem's Temple through the streets of Rome, carrying them away from Israel. If you have seen it yourself, or know about the image that I am describing, then you know that in the procession there is one frame to which your eye is drawn: the seven-branched candelabra, the *menorah*, the icon of Jewish destiny, shown as a trophy in enemy hands following the destruction of the Temple in 70 CE. It shook me to my very core to see it with my own eyes, testimony of one of the darkest hours of Jewish history, our sacred Jewish objects depicted as plunder in the non-Jewish archeological record.

This morning, I want to give a different sort of sermon from my usual – more of history lesson than anything else – about the *menorah* from ancient times to Titus to today. It is a traditional sermon in that it begins with the *parashah*, but our goal in these few minutes is to track the *menorah*, real and imagined, in all its vicissitudes. And maybe, just maybe, after this morning you will never look at a *menorah* – and perhaps even Jewish identity – in quite the same way.

We are first introduced to the *menorah* in this week's Torah reading. "You shall make a lampstand of pure gold ... Six branches shall issue from its sides; three branches from one side of the lampstand and three branches from the other side of the lampstand." The central shaft where the branches are joined together forms the seventh branch. (Exodus 25:31ff) While the size of the *menorah* is unclear, and nobody really knows what it looked like beyond the description in these biblical verses, its pride of place in the desert tabernacle was clear, its light representing God's continuous and radiant presence. As today's *haftarah* relates, it was King Solomon who built the first Temple, beginning 480 years following the Exodus from Egypt. This new permanent structure was on a larger and grander scale than the more modest desert original, and along with other upgrades to the initial design, King Solomon increased the number of *menorot* from one to ten.

It is here that the story of the *menorah* really begins in earnest. According to Rabbinic legend, when the First Temple was destroyed by the Babylonians in 586 BCE, the *menorah* was hidden away, to be brought back by the exiles after their sojourn by the rivers of Babylon. More likely, the historians explain, when the Second Temple was built following the first exile, the new *menorah* in the Second Temple sought to conform to earlier biblical specifications. According to the Book of Maccabees, this *menorah* was removed in 169 BCE by the archenemy of the Hanukkah story, Antiochus, until, of course, our hero Judah Maccabee replaced the stolen one after he cleansed and rededicated (in Hebrew: *Hanukkah*) the Temple.

Which brings us to the Arch of Titus itself. We know from the corroborated testimony of the Jewish historian Josephus and the Arch itself, that the *menorah* was brought to Rome and displayed as part of the triumph of Vespasian and Titus. Dedicated by the Senate and the Roman people in honor of Titus, the Arch conveys the might of the Romans. Josephus reports that Vespasian deposited the golden treasures of the Temple in the temple he had built to a goddess ironically called the Goddess of Peace. From that moment onwards the fate of the *menorah* is a mystery. From the sack of Rome, Carthage, Justinian, the Persians, the Arabs – who knows? We have no record of its continued existence. When I stayed in the Vatican last week, I was kind of hoping it would be sitting there in my room waiting for me after two thousand years, but given the new carry-on limits on international flights, I was relieved not to have to schlep it back.

What we do have, and have had all along, is the Arch of Titus. But the Arch of Titus was far more than the only depiction extant of the ancient *menorah*. The Arch conveyed the glory and victory of Rome, but for Jews it was the symbol of their defeat, submission, and tragedy. In fact, during the Middle Ages, no Jew was allowed to, or would, pass under the Arch. Instead Jews paid a fee to go through a neighboring house. In the 16th century it was at the Arch of Titus that Jews were forced to swear an oath of submission. For Jews, the Arch of Titus came to represent a world that wasn't, a world of Jewish sovereignty, Jewish self-determination and Jewish pride, a world smelted and smuggled away like the *menorah* itself.

That is pretty much how things stood for just shy of two thousand years, until February 1949, nine months after the establishment of the State of Israel. The new state was in need of an emblem – a national emblem that would represent a sovereign Jewish nation in the community of nations, an emblem that symbolized the continuity and fulfillment of the Zionist dream. A competition was announced, and 450 designs were received from 164 participants. After lengthy discussions, and in keeping with millennia of dysfunctional Jewish decision making, the committee arrived at a stalemate, threw out all the ideas and began anew. This time around, 131 submissions were received, and in the sixth meeting of the "Seal and Flag Committee," a proposal by two brothers – Maxim and Gavriel Shamir – was considered. Their sketch was a stylized menorah, a sleek decorative emblem, signaling a shift away from traditional Jewish symbols. As much as they were taken by the design offered by the Shamir brothers, the committee understood the historic weightiness of the decision at hand. Transportation Minister David Remez asked that the modern *menorah* be replaced with the *menorah* as depicted on the Arch of Titus. The message would be clear to the world. The *menorah* of Titus's triumphal procession had, for thousands of years, symbolized Jewish defeat, powerlessness, and exile. The rebirth of the Jewish state would be represented by the return and display of that very *menorah*. In place of humiliation, disgrace, and victimization would come honor, pride, and sovereignty. And so, on February 10, 1949, the Speaker of the Provisional Council of State, Joseph Sprinzak, ratified the new emblem of the State of Israel, which remains its emblem to this day. As for the Arch of Titus itself, when Ben Gurion declared independence for Israel, it is said that the Chief Rabbi of Rome gathered the entire Jewish community to walk under the arch in the opposite direction – symbolizing the return of the Jewish people to Jerusalem, to Israel, and to the dream of self determination. Finally, for those with an eye for these things, next time you go to Yad Vashem, be sure to look at Nathan Rapoport's relief "The Last March" in the main square. With a clear nod to the Arch of Titus, it depicts the return of the Diaspora Jew to Israel following the horrors of the Shoah.

David Ruderman, a historian at the University of Pennsylvania, once explained that the unique characteristic of the Jewish historical experience has been its landlessness during most of its existence. No other people, Ruderman says, has experienced the spatial and temporal discontinuities of the Jewish people, lacking a common government, language, or land. No other people, while claiming to be a definable group, has been called on to function in such vastly different contexts and under such adverse conditions. From that very first exile, to which we turn our attention in this month of Purim, Jewish identity has been hammered and sometimes hidden, subject to the capricious whims of our host culture. And yet, for all that, we have remained one people. The candelabra of our identity may extend in multiple directions, but we are – through fire and furnace – a single solid piece of metal. And that identity, a badge of otherness for so long, was transformed with the establishment of Israel to represent political honor – restored triumphantly after thousands of years of displacement, dislocation, and powerlessness.

To put it plainly, *menorot* matter. We may or may not ever know what the original *menorah* looked like. And we certainly have no reason to believe that the original *menorah* will appear sometime soon for us to reclaim it as our own. But what we do know is that as goes the *menorah*, so goes Jewish identity. From the desert wanderings to the Temple, from the Arch of Titus to the modern State of Israel, to where we put Jewish candelabras on the Upper East Side – the placement of the *menorah* is as good a litmus test as any for the Jewish condition and Jewish self perception. And thank God we are blessed to live in a time that our *menorot* are displayed proudly in our community and in the community of nations.

Or ḥadash al Tziyon ta'ir, v'nizkeh kulanu m'herah l'oro. "Cause a new light to illumine Zion, and may we all be worthy to enjoy its brightness." May we protect that flame, in our time as days before, radiating anew with an eternal promise of old.

"*Later May Be Too Late*"

This past week, along with over 13,000 other pro-Israel delegates, I attended the AIPAC policy conference. I have been going since my junior year of college when I led a delegation of fellow students. If you have never been, then you should know that it is, hands down, the largest *kiddush* you will ever see. Thousands of laypeople, Jewish professionals, clergy, Jews and non-Jews all crammed into the DC Convention Center. Congressmen and senators, policy wonks and journalists, Peres, Netanyahu, Obama, the Maccabeats, even Kathy Ireland (who still looks terrific), all to discuss, affirm, and strengthen the bonds between America and Israel. It is a "who's who" of Jewish leadership. Plenaries and breakout sessions, visits to Capitol Hill, education, and advocacy – every year it is totally energizing and a reminder to me, but more importantly to our elected officials, of the size, commitment, and coherence of the Pro-Israel Lobby.

This year, the topic of the entire conference can be distilled down to one word: Iran. From President Obama's address on Sunday to Prime Minister Netanyahu's on Monday night, with the meeting of the two taking place in between, one would never known that there was anything else to talk about. Palestinians, 1967 borders, Hamas, settlements – hardly any mention at all. All eyes were turned to Tehran's maniacal ambitions. How close are they to nuclear capability? What exactly is the threat of a nuclear Iran for Israel, for the Middle East, and for America? Are American interests and Israeli interests one and the same? If Israel strikes, should she – will she – do so only with clearance from America? With the combination of Iran's anti-Israel ideology, it and its proxies' proximity to the Jewish state, and its pursuit of the nuclear weapons, we are, without a doubt, living through one of the most precarious moments in Israel's history.

Subtlety is not really the order of the day at the Policy Conference. As at any pep rally, nuanced and textured arguments, especially in an election year, are checked at the door. But unlike the Palestinians, Jerusalem or other topics, on the question of the Iranian danger there is actually a rather broad consensus. Nobody in America or in Israel is really disputing the threat a nuclear Iran would pose to Israel and the world. Even David Grossman, perhaps the most prominent spokesmen for the Israeli left, readily stated this week, "We are dealing with the most crucial existential problem that the state of Israel may ever have faced in all its history." So what is the crux of the debate on Iran? I think the only point of discussion and difference boils down to a tactical question raised by Israeli Defense Minister Ehud Barak a few weeks ago. When sharing his concerns regarding Iran's nuclear weapons program, he stated, *"Whoever says 'later' may find that later is too late."* I think what he meant is that there are those who – while well aware of the Iranian threat – believe that we must slow down, give it time, wait for other strategies to be implemented and have their effect. Barak's comment, on the other hand, reflects an urgent sense that we are living in an "if not now, then when" moment. To delay, stall, or push off what needs to be done now misreads Iran's capabilities and underestimates Iran's intentions and will ultimately lead to our own undoing. The question is: at what point does later become too late?

To a degree, it is a debate about leadership, a debate that is hardly unique to our present moment, but rather, characterizes all junctures of decision and indecision. Though in vastly different circumstances, it is the tension felt by Aaron in his dealings with the Golden Calf. There he stood, waiting for God and Moses to wrap up their deliberations at the top of Mount Sinai, and before his very eyes the Calf was being assembled and constructed. According to the Midrash in Exodus Rabbah, Aaron tried everything he could to delay the project, thinking that Moses would return any moment and put an end to the danger. He suggested that the people give their jewelry, assuming it would buy him time. He proposed that he himself take on the building project, thinking that he could stall. He called for a festival. He did whatever he could, hoping against hope that "later" would never arrive. For all his tactics, not only did that "later" moment indeed arrive, but it arrived sooner than he anticipated, and by then it was too late. The construction of the Golden Calf was not only the darkest moment of Israel's forty-year wanderings, but was also the nadir of Aaron's prophetic career. It represented a tragic miscalculation that so many others have made since. He delayed a necessary confrontation at the critical moment of decision, thinking that he could slow down the inevitable, but the inevitable proved to be inexorable. For Aaron, later was too late, and both he and Israel paid the price.

Let me be clear about what I am saying and what I am not saying. I am *not* suggesting that Israel must presently take matters into its own hands. I am terribly troubled that in all of the posturing of this past week, there has been a deafening silence on what I believe to be a critical element of the conversation, namely: once Israel or America attacks Iran, what exactly do the next 24 hours look like? What happens when Hezbollah launches 50,000 rockets into Israel? What happens when the price of oil spikes above $200 a barrel? What happens when there is a retaliatory terrorist strike on American soil? I believe that Israel has every right to be "master of its own fate." That is, in a nutshell, the whole point of a sovereign Jewish state. As was stated with great clarity this past week, "No nation can gamble its sovereignty and security on perfect knowledge of a clandestine effort by an avowed enemy." (Howard Kohr, AIPAC Executive Director, 03.05.12) But what I would really like to hear, what I am not hearing, are brutally honest discussions on what a post-strike world looks like, and why the certainty of that terrible eventuality is preferable to the uncertainty wrought by every other dire scenario. Aaron's model of leadership may not recommend itself to us, but let's not forget that the real hero of this week's Torah reading is Moses – ready to stand in the breach, talk the Almighty down, and save Israel from certain destruction. Just because we are living through an "if not now, then when" moment, doesn't mean that we cannot move forward with thought, intention, and a bit of humility earned by our recent experiences. Sometimes the boldest leader is the one who is able to keep a cool head in the midst of a chorus counseling otherwise.

2012 is not 1938, and Iran is not Osirak. Tempting as they may be, hurling slogans, fear-mongering, and reckless bluster strike me as terribly misplaced considering the stakes at hand. Certainly our future memories of Americans and Israelis who will pay the ultimate sacrifice for present decisions should be unsullied by the crass posturing of election year politics. Again, Israel doesn't need to apologize for self-defense. As Menachem Begin stated as doctrine following Osirak, "... under no circumstances will Israel ever allow an enemy to develop weapons of mass destruction against our people." (Y. Avner, *The Prime Ministers*, p. 555) And yet, it was that same Begin who differentiated between what he called "wars of choice" and "wars of no alternative," describing '48 and '73 as the latter and, surprisingly, '67 as the former, a war of choice. In retrospect, of course, it was the necessary and right choice, but as Begin himself explained when discussing Egyptian aggression leading up to Israel's strike, "We must be honest with ourselves ... While it is indeed true that the closing of the Straits of Tiran was an act of aggression, a *casus belli*, there is always room for a great deal of consideration as to whether it is necessary to make a *casus* into a *bellum*." (R. Haass, *War of Necessity, War of Choice: A Memoir of Two Iraq Wars*, pp. 9–10) Just because striking Iran would be a war of choice does not mean it would not be well justified – now or later. But like Joshua overhearing the sounds of war coming from the camp, we need to rise above the boisterous din and insist on sober and rigorous analysis in assessing the likely costs, benefits, and consequences of every option on the table.

So what should be done and when? This Shabbat morning, let's start with the more manageable question of what you and I should do. Let me offer a lighter image, but one that hopefully provides the beginnings of the answer. On Monday, the lunch that AIPAC served was, in good Jewish fashion, Chinese food. As I was listening to the speaker, I did what I always do when eating Chinese food – I opened up my fortune cookie. The fortune read, "Your work helps ensure Israel's safety and security." While I didn't check all the other cookies, I am willing to bet that everyone else's fortune said pretty much the same thing. The symbolism of that moment for me, and I hope for all of us, is the take-home message of the conference. The stakes are too high, the window too small, the situation too grave to leave anything to fortune. Our work helps ensure Israel's safety and security. With Purim still in our rearview mirror, like Queen Esther herself, we must be responsive to our people's present needs; we dare not leave anything to chance. Sitting this round out is a decision for indecision that our people can ill afford and it is simply not an option to arrive too late.

"I have set watchmen upon thy walls, O Jerusalem, which shall never hold their peace day nor night." (Isaiah 62) May we, Americans Jews privileged to live in the company of a sovereign Israel, serve as the watchmen on her walls, neither resting nor holding our peace, vigilant and responsive to our obligations in shaping the present and future security of the Jewish State.

Va-yikra
"Elementary Forms of Religious Life"

2012 marks the one hundred year anniversary of the publication of one the most important volumes in the study of religion – Emile Durkheim's *The Elementary Forms of Religious Life*. One can rarely say that a single book defines a discipline, but in this case there is consensus that the entire field of religious studies may be understood as an extension of and reaction to Durkheim's book. Admittedly, to the world at large, the centennial of *The Elementary Forms of Religious Life* may not be in the same league as the 100th anniversary of the Oreo, but for those of us in the business, this is a very big deal.

In studying everyone from the Australian Aboriginals to the Pueblo Indians, Durkheim sought to understand the essential nature of the religious experience. His research is not only descriptive, but also a bit prescriptive. As he states in his introduction, in turning to these primitive societies, we may "arrive at an understanding of humanity as it is at present." (p. 14) For Durkheim, religion is an essential and permanent aspect of humanity. The "elementary forms of religious life" that he identifies are common to all religions no matter what era or context.

So why is this French book of religious sociology so important? Durkheim's most famous and debated claim is his contention that more than being about belief, the core of the religious enterprise is its social nature. Durkheim's defines religion as a "unified system of beliefs and practices relative to sacred things, that is to say, things set apart and forbidden – beliefs and practices which unite into one single moral community called a Church, all those who adhere to them." (p. 62) For

Durkheim, it is the collective and communal nature of religion that is key; the supernatural or spiritual dimension of religion is not his concern. All religions are equally true ... and false; faith is not the point. Religions share the basic goal of giving communities the structures, rites, and rituals to respond to common human emotions: joy, grief, thanksgiving, awe, and so on.

All this, if you took an introductory religion class in college, you may already know. What you may not know is that Emile Durkheim's name at birth was actually David Emile Durkheim and that he was the fourth child of Rabbi Moses and Melanie Durkheim, the son and grandson of rabbis. Durkheim's adoption of his middle name and his journey from a meager rabbinical home to the prestigious Sorbonne paralleled the intellectual and economic acculturation of much of French Jewry in the late 19th century. As the historian Deborah Dash Moore argues, Durkheim's scholarly contributions can best be understood in this context. It is altogether significant that Durkheim's intellectual coming of age took place when it did, in the wake of the Dreyfus trial in 1894, in which the French Jewish captain was falsely accused of treason. For Theodore Herzl, the founder of Political Zionism, it was the Dreyfus trial that spurred him to reject the promise of emancipation and turn to the establishment of a Jewish State. Durkheim's scholarship, concurrent with Herzl's activism, provided French Jewry with the language and tools to express their particularity as full participants in the revolutionary principles of liberty, equality, and fraternity. To attack a French Jew was not just an act of anti-Semitism, but an attack on the very values enshrined in French legal tradition. In words eerily applicable to the news out of France this past week, Durkheim wrote, "Whoever makes an attempt on a man's life, on a man's liberty, on a man's honor inspires us with a feeling of horror, in every way analogous to that which the believer experiences when he sees his idol profaned." Durkheim was no friend of the supernatural; he was a thoroughly assimilated Jew. With his antipathy for theology, for the ancestral rites and beliefs of his Jewish heritage, his is a religion for atheists. Yet, it was Durkheim's focus on the communal character of religion which, no less than Herzl's state, reflected an effort to help Jews, in their own eyes and the eyes of the world, integrate into the modern world without shedding their particularity. It is the rites, rituals, and ceremonies of religion that give any church (or synagogue) its sense of cohesion, its sense of purpose and place in civil society.

A case in point is our *parashah*, *Va-yikra* – the sacrificial system of Leviticus – which, while not receiving full treatment by Durkheim, would readily find a home in his schema. The rites, the cult, the sacrifices of animal and fowl, gruesome as they are, reflect a wide variety of celebrations and occasions for worship, both public and private. Thanksgiving, sin, forgiveness, festivals, purity, birth, and death – all of the ages and stages that make life, life – these are the rites that defined the Israelite community, these are the elementary forms of Israel's religious life. Of course, in a community of faith, these rituals have God at their center – an allowance that Durkheim would see as secondary at best. But even the great sage Maimonides in his *Guide for the Perplexed* sounds like a precursor to Durkheim when he explains that the object of Israel's ancient religion could not have been God, who we are told neither desired nor needed the sacrifices. The sacrificial system, according to Maimonides, bore no intrinsic significance; rather, it was only because God understood ancient Israel's need for communal worship and association that the sacrificial system was instituted and allowed. (*Guide* 3:32)

As interesting as all this may be, given that we are in a synagogue and not a university classroom, the question is not about *Va-yikra*, Maimonides, or Durkheim, but about us, a community of believers. As contemporary Jews, do we maintain our rites, rituals, and practices merely for the purpose of engendering group consciousness and intergenerational continuity? Is it conscionable for us to entertain a Judaism whose teeth derive not from an attachment to God, but an attachment to common folk practices?

Before I answer the question, you should know that such a Judaism actually has a name and a spokesman. It is called Reconstructionist Judaism and its primary spokesman is Mordecai Kaplan. Durkheim would have never believed in reincarnation, but long after Durkheim died, he did come back to life, as it were, in the thought of Kaplan, whose book *Judaism as a Civilization* repackages Judaism in Durkheim's language. Worship is not for God, but for common consciousness; religious ritual is not commanded, but a shared set of folkways; the Torah is not given by God, but a narrative passed down through the generations; *tallit, tefillin, shofar*, and *lulav* are all objects of the cult, denuded of their metaphysical significance. For that matter, Kaplan's book, written some forty years after the Dreyfus trial, reflects a sociological move similar to Durkheim's book. By framing Judaism as a system of folkways, Kaplan effectively announced American Jewry as full participants in the project called America. As evidenced by the JCC movement that is his legacy, Kaplan's articulation of Judaism bears the potential to let American Jews retain their particularity and, at the same time, lay claim to being full participants in the diverse landscape of American life.

Durkheim, Kaplan, Maimonides. These are serious names. A little humility is in order before taking issue with their claims, especially in the last few paragraphs of a sermon. And I must admit they do have a point. Every one of us who will be sitting down in just a couple of weeks for a Passover *Seder* knows that the power of ritual need not be contingent on the presence of God or on confirming the historicity of the event being commemorated. The rituals, liturgies, and traditions of our people have a hold on us, in our homes, and as a people. In so much of what we do, it is the social dimension of our Jewish practice that binds us – past, present, and future.

And yet, it is not enough. As I have said many times from this pulpit, if Judaism is presented merely as a set of folkways, functionally equivalent to any other faith or lifestyle choice, then I am not exactly sure what makes Judaism worth preserving. If my turn to religion is merely an effort to find vehicles to express joy, sorrow, awe, commitment, serenity, sin, and forgiveness, Judaism is very good, but there are certainly other religions that do it as well if not better. In addition, times are different. It is neither 1894 nor 1934. Unlike Durkheim or Kaplan, we do not need to justify ourselves as Jews to America. Rather our problem is that we need to construct a compelling argument for Jewish identity in an America all too willing to help us shed our particularity. Our faith, unlike that of Durkheim and Kaplan, needs to be assertive, confident, bold, and with a touch of the supernatural. Jewish life must not be understood as a reasonable option among many, but as an expression of our covenantal relationship with God, the core of who we are, and we can't imagine it otherwise. Embracing our own faith tightly need not interfere with someone else's ability to do the same with theirs. If anything, I think the only thing impeding American Jewry's full-throated commitment to Judaism is us – Jews.

For all this, we could say *Dayenu*, it would be enough. But the best reason I can give why Durkheim and Kaplan may be good for the classroom but not for the sanctuary is that in the quiet recesses of my heart, I am fundamentally a believer. This is my being and my heritage. Kaplan and Durkheim fail the *kishke* test. From my religion, I seek the gentle caress of the sacred, the awe of standing before God, the belief that there is in this world a set of demands that God asks of me as a Jew and as a human being. And while the totality of God's will may ever elude my reach, reach I shall – through prayer, through practice, and through study. The forms of my religious life may be elementary, they may be advanced – I don't know. But they are mine, given and asked of me by God – a God both near and far, past and present, particular and universal, a God that I set before me always, in every step of my life.

Shabbat HaGadol/Tzav
"The Uses and Abuses of History"

When the historian Peter Novick died last month, he bequeathed to the Jewish community a set of questions that will extend well beyond his years on this earth. In my years at the University of Chicago, I never studied formally with Dr. Novick, though I can clearly recall the controversy surrounding his 1999 book, *The Holocaust in American Life*. Novick, who was Jewish, contended that the Holocaust had come to play too large a role in American Jewish life. The Nazi genocide, horrific as it was, in its ubiquitous and sometimes vacuous invocation, had come to serve as "virtually the only common denominator of American Jewish identity." Furthermore, Novick claimed that history was being used by contemporary Jewry, in America and in Israel, for reasons that had nothing to do with honoring memory, but rather as a means to justify political ends. In drawing analogies between 1933, 1938, 1944 and the Six Day War, the Yom Kippur War or I suppose, even our present moment, the promiscuous use of history was not only a false equivalence, not only a coarse rallying cry separate from the merits of the crisis at hand, but actually served to cheapen the atrocity itself. You can imagine the controversy stirred up by Novick's book – from strong support to sharp criticism. The questions he raised remain to this day. Be it the Holocaust, or any historical event – is there a right and wrong, an ethics in invoking the past? Can too much historical consciousness be a bad thing? Where exactly is the line between the use and abuse of history?

Usually, when we talk about the abuse of history, we mean the opposite end of the spectrum – the lack of historical awareness. In her book *Dangerous Games*, the historian Margaret Macmillan relates the tale of the writer Susan Jacoby, who overheard two men speaking in a New York bar on the evening of September 11, 2001. "This is just like Pearl Harbor," one said. "What is Pearl Harbor?" the other asked. The first man replied, "That was when the Vietnamese dropped bombs in a harbor, and it started the Vietnam War." (p. 164) Certainly in this day and age, with a twenty-four hour news cycle and attention spans as shallow as the last tweet, our Etch-a-Sketch affliction is a collective case of attention deficit disorder. The Jewish community is no different. Our concerns for the Jewish future in many ways stem from our awareness of just how tenuous the thread is to the Jewish past, how disconnected this generation is from the generation that preceded it. We need not look far to see the second child of Passover, lacking a historical sensibility and no longer deserving a place at the table. There are dangers that come with too little history, and everything we do as educators, Jewish or otherwise, seeks to address this deficiency.

But this morning, I want to talk about a different kind of abuse of history – not too little, but too much. It is perhaps an unexpected topic given the imminent arrival of Passover, our festival of history par excellence. After all, the entire *seder* – the recitation of the Exodus narrative, the songs and rituals, everything – has the goal of relaying, retaining, and preserving our history. The Haggadah exemplifies what the French sociologist Maurice Halbwachs called "collective memory," in that what a people remembers – whether it is the Alamo, the Maine, Pearl Harbor, or the Exodus – informs a people's sense of identity and mission. For no people more than the Jews, and never more than on Passover, is history's effect on group identity so evident.

And yet on this Shabbat HaGadol, I submit to you that the Passover Haggadah is instructive not just for the history it tells, but for how it tells it, not only for making that history important, but also for modeling safeguards against the abuse of that very history.

Consider the very first declaration at the *seder* table: "This is the bread of affliction that our ancestors ate … at present we eat it here, next year in Jerusalem." From the very beginning, there is a sense of continuity *and* discontinuity established between the celebrant and the history being recited. As interested as the Haggadah is in recalling the past, it is equally interested in the muscle group needed to differentiate one moment from the next. And the question is not merely *Ma Nishtana*, why this night is different from other nights, but why this moment is distinct from other ones. Think about the oldest core text of the Haggadah (which, incidentally, most of us skip over): "Go forth and inquire what Laban intended to do to our father Jacob." In the very next line, the text explains that while in every generation enemies have risen against us, the threat of Pharaoh and the threat of Laban were of altogether different magnitudes. No one moment ever exactly mirrors another. Of course the whole point of the Haggadah is to create a sense of unbroken continuity from one generation to the next, but if you read the text very carefully, you will see that never ever does time collapse on itself. The present celebrant is always aware of his or her existence between a past exodus and a future redemption. Every Jew must see him or herself *ke'ilu*, "as if," s/he came out of Egypt. *Ke'ilu*, "as if," not exactly like. Why? Because we didn't actually go through it ourselves. We draw on that history and identify with it, but also embrace the fact that we are not that history. In fact, it is arguably this distancing, this awareness that "that was then and this is now" which is the whole point. The ability to refract the lessons of a past experience onto our present condition, but not conflate the two, that is the pedagogic lesson of the entire Passover exercise.

The Haggadah is instructive because it reminds us that as important as history may be, so too is the ability to recognize the differences between our own moment and that past. Far too often the past is used by the present in ways that obfuscate our present concerns. I am reminded of the old story of Abe and Sadie who go into couples therapy and Abe complains that whenever they argue, Sadie becomes historical. The therapist interrupts, "You mean hysterical." "No," says Abe, "historical – she's always digging up the past." This is exactly what we risk doing as Jews – worrying about a lack of history but actually suffering from some sort of historical stress disorder whereby the past becomes a stick to drive present agenda. Telling a young Jew that she or he must remain Jewish so as not give Hitler a posthumous victory will, at best, draw a blank stare and at worst, cause that Jew to turn away from this people mired in the past. Setting present policy, here in

America or in Israel, on nothing more than a mantra of "never again" lacks intellectual, moral, and tactical integrity. As much as we may wish it to be otherwise, one generation cannot hold another generation accountable for lacking a historical sensitivity that can only be acquired by having lived through the events of an era during which they were not yet born. Some people remember Kennedy being shot, some people don't. Some people lived through the Six Day War; others didn't. None of us choose to be born into the era in which live. It just works out that way and our sensibilities differ accordingly. The Haggadah insists that each generation forge a link one to the other and learn from a shared past, but it does not ask that we elide our generational differences. There is a point when fetishizing the past, be it a glorious golden age or a tragic calamity, borders on idolatry; we ignore the inexorable tug of the future at our peril. Any forward-looking agenda for the Jewish world needs to do what the creators of the Haggadah understood long ago, namely, to recognize that our moment is both connected to and different from the one before and, for that matter, the one to come. It is in that connection and difference that the secret to Jewish continuity lies.

With Passover just around the corner, there is no time like the present to think about the Jewish past. History, suggests Macmillan, if it is used with care, is important in that it provides context for our present, gives us alternatives to consider and most importantly, warns us of what might go wrong. But history does not provide answers; it can only help us form the questions we need to ask. As the British historian John Arnold wrote, "Visiting the past is something like visiting a foreign country: they do some of the things the same and some things differently, but above all else they make us more aware of what we call home."

Far too often we understand history, to use E.H. Gombrich's image, like a person standing between two mirrors, with the result that we see a great long line of mirrors, each one showing an image identical to the one before. Such a house of mirrors does a disservice to us, our past, and our future. History is better described as a moving stream into which we can never step twice (Heraclitus) or as Mark Twain reportedly said, "History does not repeat itself, at most it rhymes." This year, remember, the measure of a good *seder* is not just what we remember, but what we learn, the degree to which we engage with the past for the purpose of bringing our present into sharper focus. We ask question after question after question, questions about the past, questions that shed light on the present, questions that will help us find a brighter future.

Eighth Day Pesaḥ, Yizkor
"Round 'em Like Mantle"

When it comes to counting the Omer, the days between the second night of Pesah and Shavuot, I count the days according to different professional athletes and their jersey numbers. Two days ago, day 5: Albert Pujols. Yesterday, day 6: Bill Russell, Lebron James or, if you like, Dr. J. Today: Day 7, means one name and one name only: Mickey Mantle. Now Mickey Mantle had more vices than I care to list, and he himself was quick to point out that as a role model, he should stand as an example of what not to do and how not to act. But there was one thing that he did – that he became known for – from which I think we can all learn. If you can recall, or if you have ever seen footage of him rounding the bases after hitting a home run, he would do so with his head down, shoulders limp. No fist pump, no self-aggrandizing strut in his stride. At that moment of achievement, at the moment of triumph, he comported himself, well, like a *mensch*. Maybe it was because he didn't want to show up the pitcher; maybe it was because he knew that his next at bat could easily be a strikeout – I don't know. But maybe something in that self-deprecating jog around the bases reflected an awareness of where he came from – the idea that even at our moments of glory, we never forget our modest origins – and if you know a bit about Mantle, an Oklahoma boy from a coal mining family, nobody had origins more humble.

If there is a message of Passover, a message for this moment of Yizkor, it is the request that we, as it were, round the bases like Mantle. What I mean by this is that even at our moment of redemption, even at the time of our greatest victory, we keep our head down, we don't stick out our chests, we always remember our origins, which for us are as modest as they come.

Think about the *sedarim* that we celebrated this past week. The reminder of our humble beginnings is repeated over and over again. "This is the bread of affliction," "our father was a wandering Aramean," "from the beginning our ancestors were idol worshippers." It is remarkable that the *seder*, which has the ostensible goal to communicate the thrilling story of our redemption from Egypt, should repeatedly reference our earliest pre-redemptive beginnings. Yes, we celebrate our liberation. And yes, we are grateful that we are free, but we never forget that once we were not. Even at the height of our joy, we always remember our roots, we always remember where we came from, we never become so enthralled with our miraculous liberation that we become untethered from where it all began.

Passover teaches that the act of visiting our origins is actually the key to opening the door to our present and future. As for Moses going out to see his brethren that fateful day, to remember where you came from is actually the first step towards a future redemption. It is not that we seek a return to some long-gone yesteryear; after all, we are happy and filled with gratitude for our present blessings. But a reminder of where we came from is the rudder that steadies us as we steer towards the future.

For me, much of the thrill of being home for *sedarim* was exactly this – the reminder that who I am today is an extension of and a reaction to my beginnings. When you sit at your parents' *seder* for Passover, with your brothers and sisters-in-law and your children in attendance, your sense of perspective radically shifts. In my case, I sat where my mother told me to, I cleared the dishes when I was told to do so, and I tried to keep my kids moderately well-behaved. From Jewish day school, to Jewish studies, to rabbinical school, to a doctorate, more money has been poured into my Jewish education than is helpful to count, but at my father's *seder* you better believe that I only read when I am called on to do so. And frankly, I wouldn't have it any other way – for a day or two. That is the table at which my Jewish identity took shape. I don't live at that table, I don't seek to return to it, but that visit, that reminder of where it all began, is critically important to keeping me moored. It reminds me that I am who I am only because I had the blessing of beginning where I began. Mark Twain once quipped that a self-made man is about as likely as a self-laid egg. A return to one's origins is more than a nostalgic walk down memory lane. To return to one's origins has the effect of both expanding and narrowing your lens of self perception. It puts focus on what really matters, on who and why we are who we are, and for what we are truly grateful.

Which is exactly what this moment of Yizkor is about. We return to the tables that gave us life, only in this case, the journey comes by way of the gift of memory. Yizkor is our chance, for a brief moment in time, to visit the memories of those we love and who loved us most. Whether years have gone by, or the loss is recent, the mothers, fathers, brothers, sisters, husbands and wives, sons and daughters we recall are the ones who made us who we are. Yizkor gives us permission to recall a few of the hundreds if not thousands of memories that have made us who we are today. It reminds us that none of us are self-made. We are all extensions of and reactions to the tables of our past, without which we would not be who we are. I suspect that for most of us, these memories are the most quiet and intimate sort, memories held privately and tenderly – quiet conversations, life lessons learned, years of partnership, the model of a life we seek to emulate or perhaps the shattered reality of a love taken too soon. Today we recall not the titles or awards, but the loving lives of quiet dignity, the relationships of infinite worth to which we return at this time.

There are those who go into the great outdoors, or to meditation retreats, or elsewhere to find their center. This is well and good, but the Jewish way to get our bearings is Yizkor. Some of us come from humble origins, some of us don't. Some of us have realized our dreams, some of us chase them without respite. Yizkor reminds us what really matters. It reminds us how we should lead our lives, because after all, it reminds us, that some day, please God, someone will recite Yizkor for us and, I promise you, it will not be fancy titles that they will remember.

Last week I had a meeting with a major figure in New York life. His office sits at the top of a big building with views of the entire city, with multiple assistants running around, an anteroom filled with pictures of famous people, and more signs of being a *macher* than I can list. My host greeted me and must have seen that I was a bit starstruck by it all. He said: "You know, Rabbi, I always remind myself that at the end of all this, there are only four people who will be saying *kaddish* for me." It was a beautiful sentiment for me, this man somehow embodying

Kipling's comment that while some of us may walk with kings, one must never lose the common touch. Aware of our own mortality, we realize that what really matters are the relationships by which we will be remembered. It is the very knowledge that our time in this world is limited that reminds us, again and again, that no matter who we are, no matter what our station in life may be, we always round the bases like Mantle. We always remember where we came from and we never forget the shared fate that awaits us all.

I began with a story about one number, and I will conclude with a story about another number, one of my favorites – number 36. According to rabbinic tradition, the characteristic most associated with the number 36 is humility. Talmudic legend tells that there are 36 people, called the *Lamed-vavniks – lamed*, the Hebrew letter for 30 and *vav*, the letter for 6. Thirty-six people who live quiet, unassuming lives, whose righteousness is of such a noble quality that without them, the world itself would cease to exist. Nobody knows who they are - most importantly, not even the *Lamed-vavniks* themselves. To think that one is, or God forbid, to declare oneself to be a *Lamed-vavnik*, would result in immediately forfeiting the claim, because such lack of humility would be a sure sign that you are not worthy of the name.

For all of their praiseworthiness in this world, the tradition tells us nothing about the *Lamed-vavniks* in death. Perhaps for us at this moment of Yizkor, we will grant that those being remembered today are, at least for each of us, the individuals without whom *our* worlds would not exist. Their love, their commitments, their lives granted us the ability to be who we are. We are grateful, we never forget them and in their passing, we assign them the status that is their due.

And here in this world, who knows? Our deeds in the years ahead will tell the story. The best we can do, the only thing we can do, is to seek to lead lives of modest and humble compassion, to keep our heads down as we round 'em, acting with love and kindness to those who matter most and who are most dependent on our care, so that we, in the generations to come, will, like those we remember today, be remembered for a blessing.

Eighth Day of Pesaḥ, Remarks
"On the Freedoms and Limits of the Pro-Israel Dialogue"

In retrospect, in deciding to share my thoughts on the freedoms and limits of the Pro-Israel dialogue, I probably should not have chosen to speak after *Adon Olam* and before Kiddush. Indeed, if one of the lessons learned from all this is that timing "matters," then how much more so when your remarks are the only thing standing between a three-hour service and lunch?

It occurs to me that in this room right now there may be both those who are anxiously anticipating my comments and those who have no idea what is going on. So let me manage expectations by stating that which you may take as good news, bad news, or a combination of both. My remarks this morning will not be as expansive as you may have expected. There are times in this world when less is more, and this is one of them. From the moment I decided that I would speak today, there have been days that I wanted to give an impassioned critique of Peter Beinart's views in anticipation of his upcoming visit; and there have been other days that I believed that what I really should do was give a full-throated defense of his position. But then something really interesting happened; the more I wrote and rewrote this speech in my head, the less and less ground it covered. Because I realized that my responsibility as the rabbi of this congregation is not give a book review, not to defend or critique an invited speaker, an activity that I have not done with anyone else. Rather I decided that I want to use this time to explain how we got here, what we stand for as a congregation, and how this moment, in all its complexity, is actually an incredible opportunity for growth and communal self definition. Because, at its core, I do not think that this conversation is about the strengths or weaknesses of Beinart's book. I believe there are greater principles at stake, principles that we need to articulate and affirm as a congregation, principles that both now and in the years to come are worthy of our most vigorous defense.

Let's start, as the song goes, at the very beginning, or at least the beginning of when I arrived here at Park Avenue Synagogue. I made a commitment that this congregation would stand at the center of the most pressing conversations on the Jewish docket. Whether it is the state of congregational music, the condition of supplementary Jewish education, the future of Conservative Judaism, or the nature of the Diaspora-Israel relationship, Park Avenue Synagogue would be the place where these conversations happen. The speakers we bring in, the programs and schools under our watch, the lay and professional leadership together would understand their mission to be the relentless effort to identify and address the major challenges facing the Jewish world. Within our walls we would generate the transformational thinking that would contribute towards the revitalization of this community and serve as a model for the rest of the Jewish world. It is big, it is bold, audacious and ambitious and I am happy to say – now heading into my fifth year – we are well on our way.

This year, through the generosity of a congregational family that is as anonymous as it is generous, we began an annual lecture series, whose stated mission is to bring top scholars and notable intellectuals to speak to a topic that we believe to be a priority issue facing the Jewish future. We are in the midst of determining the theme of next year's series, and if you want input, then I invite you to get involved in the synagogue. I can clearly recall two happenings that directly impacted the choice of topic for this year. First, a re-emergence in Israel of the "who is a Jew" question in Israeli life – a question that should be of profound concern for the members of this congregation. And second, the piece Peter Beinart published in the *New York Review of Books* in 2010 on a perceived generational distancing of American Jewry from Israel, an article in which he asserted that for a certain segment of American Jewry, rather than being a source of solidarity, Israel had become a point of alienation. Whatever you or I may have thought of his thesis, the brouhaha surrounding the piece signaled the rawness of the nerve that it touched. These events, along with my ongoing commitment that our community stand at the forefront of Israel education and engagement both now and in the generations to come, led to the theme for this year's series: "Israel in the American Jewish Imagination." The flyers were on your seats on Rosh Hashanah. The pamphlet blurb asks the question plainly: "Can North American Jewry be political and philanthropic stakeholders in Israel's wellbeing and simultaneously voice criticism of the country it defends so vigorously? How shall non-Orthodox Diaspora Jewry hold close a Jewish state that does not embrace or even recognize the Jewishness of its most ardent supporters?" The goal of the series was to create a year-long forum, as stated, "to invite representatives from across the political spectrum to share recommendations on how to move forward, with an eye towards helping our community express its own voice in this critical conversation."

To review the year thus far: We have had Leon Wieseltier, Steven Cohen, Daniel Gordis, Dan Senor, and Natan Sharansky, and on May 8 we will have Donniel Hartman. While not formally part of the series, much of our synagogue programming has also been directed to this theme. Ambassador Ido Aharoni addressed us on Rosh Hashanah; Alan Dershowitz spoke to us in the fall; we hosted an event where Bret Stephens spoke; and we reached out to everyone from Prime Minister Netanyahu, to President Shimon Peres, to the former head of the opposition Tzipi Livni, to Ambassador Ron Prosor of the United Nations and beyond. We have a congregational trip to Israel planned for the weekend of Memorial Day and Shavuot, a *Bnei Mitzvah* family trip in December, and a young family trip already filling up for June 2013. There is much more that I could list, but the point is that we are doing exactly what we set out to do: to raise the level of conversation, to encounter voices that do not merely parrot the beliefs we would hold anyway; in other words, to think critically about critical issues, thereby fulfilling not only our mandate to be at the center of conversations facing the Jewish world, but also to serve as a model of creative and inclusive thinking for the Jewish future. When it comes to engaging in the relationship between Diaspora Jewry and Israel, you can be proud of your *shul*, a *shul* that, by the way – through the generous donations of people in this room – is also funding a Birthright trip, so that every single young person who grew up in this community and others will have the opportunity to make a first – and please God, not final – trip to Israel.

And, yes, it did occur to us to invite Peter Beinart, the individual whose 2010 article was part of the impetus for our lecture series. The invitation was issued, the date was set – all confirmed last summer. And lest there be any intrigue, barring any changes in his personal schedule, he will be speaking here on April 27 following our musical Kabbalat Shabbat services.

In the meantime, Peter Beinart wrote an article in *The New York Times* and subsequently released his book, *The Crisis of Zionism*. Since then, many people have reached out to me by phone, email, and in person asking how it is we can host him. By hosting him, are we not somehow giving tacit support for his position, a position that some – but not all – find problematic and objectionable.

It is a fair question, and it is a question to ask not only of Beinart but of all speakers at Park Avenue Synagogue, a question to which I feel compelled to respond.

There is a short answer and a longer answer. The short answer is no. In inviting a speaker here, neither I personally, nor we institutionally are signaling agreement with that person's positions. I have certainly disagreed with many of the comments made by speakers this year, both their published writing and what they have said on their visits. I can readily recall multiple occasions sitting in dialogue with different guests, responding to their remarks with respectful critique and on at least a few occasions, exasperation. To book someone as a speaker does not mean that we endorse a position. To be sure, there are occasions when speakers absolutely do reflect the mission of the synagogue. A good example is next Shabbat when Chancellor Arnold Eisen of the Jewish Theological Seminary will address the community. Chancellor Eisen, unlike other speakers, is allowed to do something nobody else does – to speak to a captive audience on a Friday night or Shabbat morning. An invitation to Chancellor Eisen reflects my personal belief and our institutional policy that our commitments to JTS are part and parcel of what this community stands for. I don't want to say never, but I try my darnedest not to have opinions that do not reflect the institutional mission of the synagogue voiced during a prayer service.

Whether it is Beinart, Wieseltier, Gordis or anyone else, it strikes me as both ungracious and unfair to impose such an encounter on an unsuspecting congregant who has come to *shul* for spiritual uplift.

Another, but not insignificant point. You may also have noticed that with all of the Israel education and engagement, I have left out one dimension – advocacy. Our guests, though I have heard them speak elsewhere on behalf of AIPAC, J Street or other organizations, are not invited here to forward the mission of another agency. To say it another way, you may have noticed that we have not had an Israel advocacy event in the building during my tenure. To be sure, this is a very prickly issue for me. Why? Because as I have said over and over (and all my sermons are on our website), education, engagement, and Israel travel are not enough. To live as a Jew in this time and not understand Israel advocacy as a constituent element of your Jewish identity, is to miss out on the fullness of what it means to be a contemporary Jew. Since long before I arrived here, I have been making my personal and philanthropic commitments to Israel advocacy. I am proud of my decisions. They reflect my political sensibilities, and I call on each of you to do the same. But that is where the statement ends. As the rabbi of a 1500-family congregation, I am the rabbi, as it were, of both the red states and the blue states. There is a trust that comes with being the rabbi of this congregation, a promise that our mailing list does not become fodder for other organizations, no matter how noble their intentions may be. Again, I don't want to say never, because if I have learned anything, I have learned that I am learning all the time, but the present policy that the advocacy choices individuals in this congregation make remain the choices of those individuals is a policy that reflects my views and those of the leadership of the congregation. It is a policy that is here to stay for the foreseeable future.

And so, with all of the qualifications out of the way, we can go to the heart of the matter – the long answer to the question: Who is and who isn't allowed to speak at our *shul*? Our synagogue is not a college campus; this is not a First Amendment issue. We are allowed to make choices as to who is allowed to speak and who isn't.

When it comes to Israel, the range of conversation can be defined as those who advocate for a **secure, *Jewish, and democratic state***. Secure – because for me, the safety and well being of Jews is non-negotiable.

Jewish – because while there are those who would trade Israel's Jewish character for another value, I will not. Our prayers for Israel exist on the backs of thousands of years of Jewish longing and the Jewishness of the state is non-negotiable. Democratic – there are those who would create a state that does not acknowledge the rights of all its citizens and those people are not invited to speak in our synagogue. And finally, a state: there are those both at the extreme end of the Jewish world, and of course, in the non-Jewish world, who do not recognize the right of the Jewish state to exist; they have no place in our communal conversation. That is it. Those are the boundaries: a secure, Jewish, democratic state. You may agree, you may disagree; you may believe these boundaries to be overly constrictive or excessively loose, but that is as close as I can get to defining the limits and freedoms of our Israel dialogue. It is the Zionist dream as articulated by Theodore Herzl. It is just as compelling and urgent and defensible today as it was when he first articulated it.

I have read Peter Beinart's book from cover to cover. I have many opinions about it, but I believe that it exists well within these boundaries that I have laid out. Some of the comments that I have received have suggested that Beinart is anti-Zionist, a self-hating Jew, somehow an enemy of the Jewish state and the Jewish people. I don't know Peter Beinart; to the best of my knowledge we have never met. But I can tell you that from what I have read, he is totally invested in working towards furthering a secure, Jewish, democratic state. You may believe that he is wrong and misguided, or that his recommendations come at too great a cost for Israel. I invite you to engage with him respectfully when he comes here. But the words "anti-Jewish" and "anti-Zionist" are words that strike me as totally inapplicable. To bandy them about is to diminish the integrity of the dialogue we are committed to creating.

We are living through a very delicate moment for Israel. Israel is facing existential threats from Iran, from her neighbors all around, and in the court of world opinion. Israel does not lack for external threats and each one of us has an obligation to stand vigilant on Israel's behalf. But there is another danger, a danger that we face from within, right here in America, in New York, and in our own community. Somehow we have found ourselves unable to countenance an opinion that is not our own, and when we do, rather than engaging it, confronting it, and even arguing with it, we simply label it as beyond the bounds of acceptable discourse. From the political left to the right, there are Jews calling other Jews *treif*. In just a few weeks, the Jewish community of New York will be marching down Fifth Avenue in support of Israel. Sunday, June 3, to be exact, and I expect all of you come out that day in force. I am deeply concerned by those who have called on the organizers of the Celebrate Israel parade to bar progressive pro-Israel organizations from participating. As if the Jewish community needs more *tsuris*, somehow it is now in vogue for Jews to declare those with whom we disagree as untouchable. We are perilously close to the closing of the Jewish mind, losing our ability to sit down with anyone who holds opinions different from our own. We listen only to those whom we want, our information bubbles filter the rest out, and we grow narrower day by day.

It is for this reason that it is so very important that our community continues to model the example that we have set. The late, great Rabbi Arthur Hertzberg explained that "One cannot affirm one's own certainties without understanding the counter certainties of others." When we invite a speaker to Park Avenue Synagogue – and more importantly, when you choose to listen to that speaker – it does not signal weakness, it signals strength. It tells the world that the opinions you hold, whatever your politics may be, are held with confidence because you have encountered and withstood the counterclaims of the other. We can learn much from the great rabbinic debates of Hillel and Shammai. Hillel, tradition explains, won the debates not merely due to his intellectual prowess. Hillel won because in stating his opinion he always began by first stating the opinion of Shammai, his loyal opposition. Moreover, the tradition teaches that the houses of Hillel and Shammai, though differing on basic interpretations of Jewish law, still married their children one to the other, studied each other's opinions and acknowledged each other as members of the House of Israel. To be a flagship community means that we have both the responsibility and opportunity to model behavior worthy of being followed by others. I believe that this moment, here and now, is such an opportunity to demonstrate that we are a community capable of engaging with the full range of the pro-Israel discussion. Whether you decide to come or not, what happens between now and Peter Beinart's visit on April 27, what happens on the evening itself, and, more importantly, what happens in the years that follow, will not speak just to this or that position, but will speak to our community's ability to live up to the highest ideals of our tradition.

As I wrote in anticipation of today, if there is a take-home message from this holiday of Passover, just hours away from concluding, it is the inclusive nature of the Jewish conversation. The Jewish family is made up of different voices, from the wise, to the wicked, to the simple, to the one who does not know how to ask. More important than the labels is the realization that each one of them, year in and year out, returns to sit at the table. So too our congregational table. As the saying goes: "Wherever we stand, we stand with Israel." From the left to the right, we are working together to find a path forward, all of us unflinching in our commitment to a secure, Jewish, democratic state.

Aḥarei Mot/K'doshim
"True Grit"

Whether in reference to Yonatan, the fallen hero of the raid on Entebbe, or Bibi, the present Prime Minister of Israel, the Netanyahu name has long evoked an image that is both gutsy and altogether original. But even before the sons, it was their father, Benzion, who with his path-breaking work first bestowed the Netanyahu name with its daring inflections. Indeed, with this week's passing of Dr. Benzion Netanyahu at the age of 102, the field of Jewish history has lost one of its most important and iconoclastic scholars. Netanyahu's scholarship ranged from a book-length biography of the famed fifteenth-century Spanish scholar and statesman Don Isaac Abravanel, to a 1400-page tome on the origins of the Spanish Inquisition, to recent surveys of foundational Zionist thinkers. His contributions are important not just for their breadth and depth, but because of the boldness with which he called on historians to reconsider long held assumptions. As impressive as his scholarship, his interests transcended mere academic inquiry; in his writings, one can sense that Netanyahu believed his observations about the Jewish yesteryear were consequential for the Jewish present and future. Early in his career, he served as secretary to Ze'ev Jabotinsky, the leader of the Revisionist Zionist movement and ideological godfather to the secular right wing of Israeli politics.

Given the impossible task of summarizing such a career in one sermon, this morning I want to focus on one scholarly claim Netanyahu made, a claim that at first may seem trifling and perhaps even insignificant, but will show itself to raise profound and vexing questions for all of us living in the shadow of this towering historian of blessed memory.

Until Netanyahu, there was basically one dominant theory about the Marranos of 15th-century Spain. Forcibly converted to Christianity, the Marranos – also known as Christianos Nuevos (New Christians) – were believed by historians to have, at great personal risk, continued to practice Judaism in secret. The Spanish Inquisition, in a sentence, was understood as the effort to ferret out these crypto-Jews unlawfully practicing the faith of their ancestors.

In examining the evidence, Netanyahu arrived at a different assessment. While state pressure may well have resulted in the forced conversions of the Jews, the Marranos were not only *not* practicing their Judaism secretly, but they were sincere Christians – totally detached from Judaism and delightfully immersed in their Christian faith. Contrary to what had previously been claimed, the Inquisition and its *auto-da-fés* arose not to eradicate suspected Jewish heresy, but rather because the old Christians saw that these New Christians, in acclimating to Spanish society, were now rising to distinguished positions. The persecution of the Jews, according to Netanyahu, had nothing to do with investigating and punishing covert observance of Judaism. Rather it was a racially motivated attempt to rid the Iberian peninsula of anyone of Jewish origin and blood.

Netanyahu drew on both Jewish and non-Jewish literature from his time. One fortuitously timed example comes from this week's *parashah* – the commandment in Leviticus 18 that the Israelites should copy neither the practices of the Egyptians whence they had come, nor those of the Canaanites whither they were headed. Altogether telling is the comment made by our previously mentioned 15th-century commentator, Don Isaac Abravanel, who, in explaining this verse, cites Maimonides' understanding of human nature that it is in the nature of people to be drawn into the thoughts and deeds of their neighbors and the norms of their nation. Netanyahu understood that in the ancient Israelites, Abravanel saw a cautionary precedent for the behavior that he himself witnessed in his own days, the tug to assimilate into the dominant culture. As Abravanel, who lived through the Inquisition and Expulsion, understood all too well, Netanyahu would contend that despite the Jews' feeling at home in their host culture and faith, the host culture and faith would never feel comfortable hosting a people who in their eyes would forever be interloping Jews.

And here, of course, we enter into the heart of the matter. My "aha" moment on Netanyahu came when I was reading a short introduction he wrote not about Abravanel or the Spanish Inquisition, but about the 19th-century Russian Zionist thinker Leon Pinsker. Netanyahu explained that in 19th-century Russia, unlike 15th-century Spain, the path to Jewish assimilation came not by way of forced conversion, but by way of enlightenment and emancipation. Nevertheless, as in Spain, the Russian Jewish community would receive a rude awakening by way of persecution – pogroms that reminded the Jews that try as they might, Jews would never find acceptance in the Diaspora. As Netanyahu tells it, Pinsker's brand of Zionism represented the belief that it was those Jews who deluded themselves into thinking that they would be accepted by their enlightened hosts who would receive the rudest and most painful wake-up call. To use the image offered by Pinsker's hero Israel Zangwill at the time of the Kishinev pogroms, it was the Jews who sought to protect themselves by putting Russian sacred images in their windows who would be the people especially chosen for persecution.

I don't know enough about Spanish or Russian Jewish history to weigh in on the particulars, but let me connect the dots as I see them. Netanyahu's characterizations of Spanish and Russian history were not just about Spain and Russia, but about his own moment, 20th-century Jewish history. Netanyahu lived before, during, and after the atrocities of the Holocaust. He knew exactly what had happened to European Jewry. He had seen their delusional hope for acceptance, and he lived to see "the pity of it all." Netanyahu held a grand and cyclical understanding of our people's history. Jews in the Diaspora are the proverbial frog in the frying pan; the heat may gradually increase, but we stay right there, thinking we can adapt and adjust until we succumb and die. Furthermore, there is a direct line between Netanyahu's observations about Diaspora Jewry and his service to Jabotinsky's brand of Zionism. For Jabotinsky, the Diaspora yields one of two possible outcomes, assimilation or persecution. Jabotinsky prophetically proclaimed to Diaspora Jewry of 1937, "Eliminate the Diaspora, or the Diaspora will surely eliminate you." As for the stories Diaspora Jews like to tell about the Marranos and their descendants lighting candles generations later – they are sentimental, self-serving, and delusional.

The Diaspora is better described as an ironclad melting pot that will make Jews either indistinguishable from or insufferable to the *goyim*, or more likely, both.

Netanyahu's assessment is, to say the least, a difficult pill to swallow. All of us in this room have staked our future on the viability of a Jewish life in the Diaspora and nobody wants to be told that one's life's work and reason for being is a lost cause. But just because it is an uncomfortable question doesn't permit us to avoid it. After all, can you name a single Jewish Diaspora community in the last 3000 years that did not end either with assimilation or persecution? Because in Netanyahu's schema, these are the only options: assimilation, nationalism, or rejection ... persecuted even as we proclaim ourselves at home among those who shun us.

I don't have an easy answer, but perhaps we can begin with the acknowledgment that Netanyahu's version is only one of many tellings of Jewish history, each one with an ideological ax to grind. You see, a historian's ordering of the past, like that of a teenager stumbling home long past curfew, is an act of self-justification that can have as much (or as little) to do with the truth as suits his or her purpose. Krochmal, Geiger, Graetz, Dubnow, Buber, there are as many versions of history as there are historians. One great example to counter Netanyahu is Simon Rawidowicz,who wrote an essay called "Israel – the Ever Dying People." He contended that anyone "who studies Jewish history will readily discover that there was hardly a generation in the Diaspora that did not consider itself the final link in Israel's chain." The First Temple, the Second Temple, Rabbi Akiva, Brenner, Berditchevsky – for thousands of years, every Jewish generation has believed that it is the final generation of Jews, only to discover: *yesh tikvah l'aharitekh*, there is hope beyond you. The last 60-plus years in America have been some of the most intellectually, culturally, politically and economically exciting and curious years of Jewish history – period. Synagogues, UJAs, seminaries, JCCs, Jewish studies departments, entire universities ... The Beastie Boys. Even were you to exclude the miracle that is the modern State of Israel, it is accurate to say that to be a Jew in America today is to know blessings that no Jew at any other time of Jewish history could have imagined possible. The fact that this era comes immediately in the wake of the Holocaust – the darkest moment of our people's history – only makes it that much more remarkable. Are there problems? Of course there are. But anyone with an inkling of the road we have traveled knows that the problems we face are the kind of problems that any other generation would have loved to have.

So who is right? Netanyahu? Ravidowicz? Is the bottom about to fall out, or are our brightest days just around the corner? Whose version of Jewish history more accurately describes our present?

The truth is that neither Netanyahu nor Rawidowicz, nor any historian of the past is entrusted to do what you and I are entrusted to do – to define the Jewish future. As Mordecai Kaplan taught: "The past or its proxies can no more pass judgment upon the present than the child can sit in judgment upon the man." (*Judaism as a Civilization*, 404.) Grand theories of history, appealing as they are, have the effect of eliding both the challenges and opportunities that define the particularities of the present. The concurrent blessings of America and the modern State of Israel make ours a *sui generis* moment. Given the choice, when it comes to the Jewish future, I would rather bet on the educated choices we make here in this room over recommendations garnered from wise and well meaning reflections on the past. True courage, true grit, true heroism of spirit lies in the belief that every Jew and every generation of Jews gets to write its own chapter, learning from our history but not being overwhelmed by it. Or as Margaret Mead would have said had she been Jewish: "Never doubt that a small group of thoughtful committed Jews can change the world … it's the only thing that ever has." It is not what happened 500 or 100 years ago that will determine the Jewish future, but what is done today – by you, by me, by all of us, equal stakeholders in our people's fate. May each of us be up to the task, blessed to be alive at this, the very moment that our destiny is knocking at our door.

Emor/Lag BaOmer
"The Caves of Our Lives"

This past Thursday, on *Lag BaOmer*, the 33rd day of the counting of the Omer, tens of thousands of Jewish pilgrims gathered in the northern Israeli town of Meron for a memorial celebration, a *Yom Hilula*, at the grave of the mystic sage Rabbi Shimon Bar Yochai. A student of the great Rabbi Akiva, Rabbi Shimon Bar Yochai emerged in the 2nd century, in the shadow of Roman persecution, as one of the great scholars of his generation. An original thinker and generator of Jewish law, Bar Yochai is perhaps best known for having the authorship of the foundational Kabbalistic text – the Zohar – attributed to him. Throughout Israel this week, and especially at his burial site, there are dancing, bonfires, and festivities, all in his name.

In honor of the occasion, this morning I would like to share with you the most famous Bar Yochai story. Strange as the story is, you will come to see that is not only about him and his mystical journey, but about each and every one of us, and our own aspirations in the religious journeys of our lives.

The Talmud (BT Shabbat 33b–34a) recounts that one day Bar Yochai and his colleagues were sitting in dialogue reflecting on the building projects of the Roman empire – the bathhouses, the bridges, the marketplaces – everything the Romans had built. While one rabbi complimented the Romans and another sat silent, Bar Yochai critiqued them, contending that the Roman projects provided no greater societal good, serving only the vanity of the Romans themselves. Unbenownst to the group, an informer sat in their midst who reported their conversation to the authorities. A decree of death was levied on our yet-to-be-mystic. Fearing for his life, Bar Yochai hid in a cave with his son Rabbi Elazar. Sustained only by a miraculous carob tree and spring of water, they lived in that cave for twelve years. Every day, they immersed themselves not just in the sand but in study, prayer, and reflection, isolated from everyone and everything. Twelve years passed, Caesar died, and the decree against Bar Yochai was annulled. Elijah the Prophet appeared and informed Bar Yochai and his son that that it was now safe for them to emerge from the cave. And here is where, if it isn't already, the story gets a little weird. Brimming with piety from his monastic cave existence, Bar Yochai is shocked to discover life on the outside going on – business as usual. Bar Yochai simply cannot understand that people could plow fields, harvest crops, tend to their daily affairs – activities that in his mind were altogether earthly and transitory concerns. Filled with zeal, Bar Yochai gazes with such disgust at the world at large, that everything upon which he casts his eyes is incinerated by his glance. At this point – and hold on to this point – a heavenly voice reprimands him for the destruction that he is wreaking and commands him to go back into the cave to cool off. Twelve months later, a voice calls him back into the world once again. To make a long story a little shorter, with his fiery gaze simmered down, Bar Yochai goes on to be one of the great teachers of Torah of our people. He builds public works projects, he serves the Jewish community, he becomes a great mystical teacher, and, in case you are wondering, he even has his revenge on the one who informed on him in the first place.

Sometimes, a story is just a story and a cave is just a cave. But as I was telling Bar Yochai's story to the kids this year, I started to ask myself for the first time whether this cave represented more than just a cave, and if Bar Yochai shuttling in and out of the cave is about more than a rabbi hiding from oppressive authorities. After all, be it rabbinic literature, Alice in Wonderland, the Chronicles of Narnia, Gulliver's Travels or the Indian in the Cupboard – nine times out of ten, the trip down the rabbit hole, from one reality to another, is a journey about more than physical geography and of spiritual and metaphysical consequence. These transformations are not just for children, but for all of us, commentaries on the world as it is and as it should be, what we want most, sometimes what we fear most. In a good author's hands all these elements can deftly be put into conversation in what may at first glance seem like a casual fairy tale.

And then it struck me. Long before all of these stories is the probably most famous cave story of all – the allegory of the cave bequeathed to us by Plato. You may remember it from an undergraduate philosophy class. It's a story which, if we revisit it briefly, makes the Bar Yochai story all the more interesting.

Imagine if you will, writes Plato in the voice of Socrates, a group of people who have spent their whole lives chained up in a cave unable to move. Behind them is a fire, but staring at the wall, all they can see are shadows. Having never seen or experienced anything else, they naturally mistake their existence for reality. Now what would happen, asks Socrates, if one of the cave dwellers were to be liberated. He would, says the author, go with great difficulty to the outside world and at first be overwhelmed and disoriented by the light outside the cave. After some time, the liberated prisoner would come to realize that the world that he had believed to be reality was a world of mere shadows. Ever so slowly, he would grow accustomed to the world outside the cave. Upon returning to the cave, however, this now enlightened individual would be thoroughly misunderstood, ridiculed, and even persecuted by his chained fellows; all his new knowledge would be dismissed outright. After all, these cave dwellers never experienced what he came to experience, why should they believe his fantastical stories?

This allegory, explains Plato, is the journey of the philosopher from the darkness of this world towards the Platonic ideal and then back into the real world. Plato knew that his philosopher mentor Socrates, the gadfly of the state, was – like the liberated prisoner who returned to the cave – never accepted by the world that rejected him. Of course the allegory is a commentary not just on Socrates, but on the nature of knowledge, on reality, and the degree to which any enlightened individual can return and influence those who remain dwelling in the everyday world.

All this is a very circuitous path to bring us back to Rabbi Shimon Bar Yochai. A former teacher of mine, Lee Levine, suggested that the Bar Yochai story of the Talmud was well aware of, if not inspired by, Greek philosophical myth. More recently, my colleague Charlotte

Fonrobert of Stanford has also written that given the striking parallels between Plato's cave and that of Bar Yochai, it is altogether reasonable to think that the story in the Talmud is a revision, commentary, and perhaps even criticism of Plato's allegory.

For the moment, let's set aside the questions of literary influence and take these texts as allegories for something much bigger, and consider what they say about human nature, knowledge, and the spiritual quests of our lives.

For starters, both stories seem to indicate that there are two worlds: in the cave and outside of the cave. In the Plato story, humanity exists shackled and unenlightened in the cave. In the Bar Yochai story, humanity goes about its day-to-day work outside of the cave. In both stories, an individual makes the journey from the everyday world into a world containing a higher truth – for Plato, the realm of forms and ideas; for Bar Yochai, the estoeric world of pious mysticism. In both stories, the individual who has come to possess this rarified knowledge reenters the everyday world and, in both cases, that process of re-acclimating and acceptance is unsuccessful. For Plato, the philosopher is rejected; for Bar Yochai, everything he sees is incinerated. The stories are not identical, but they do run parallel. They are stories about the acquisition of mystical or metaphysical truth, and the inability of an individual in possession of that truth to function in the world of the unenlightened.

But there is a difference – a difference that makes all the difference in the world. It is the scene at the very end. Plato's allegory concludes with the philosopher sitting uncomfortably in what is understood as an altogether inferior world of the everyday. In the Talmudic story, Bar Yochai, initially unable to return to the everyday world, is told to go back in the cave and then emerges twelve months later to begin his ministry to the community at large. To be sure, he remains a mystic. But he is also a man who learns to contribute to his people. Remember, our first contact with him was his being critical of the Roman public works. Our next snapshot was his difficulty in accommodating his piety to the everyday world. The resolution of our story is when he comes to realize that his otherworldly zeal must find application in the world. Teaching, building, family – all the things that make life, life.

Any student of religion knows that within rabbinic culture and, for that matter, any religious culture, there exists a tension as to whether the claims of one's faith should or shouldn't inform other aspects of life. If, after all, the point of religion is to transcend our worldly selves and connect to a higher truth, then there arguably exists a fundamental incompatibility between our domestic and communal existence and the claims of our religion, an incompatibility rendered evident in Plato's allegory. For Bar Yochai the take-home message is very different. The Talmudic story makes it very clear that the purpose of our faith is to impact the world around us. There may be two worlds, but the Jewish spiritual ideal is an integrated existence, where the tension between those worlds is a productive one, each world informing and influencing the other. In a sentence, it is the moment that Bar Yochai is sent back into the cave that is a critique not just of Plato's cave, but of the entire idea that one's spiritual life and one's everyday life are two separate lives.

Jewish spirituality, though not oblivious to the allure of otherworldly pursuits, is better described as the ongoing effort to bring the mystical into the everyday. As our own Milton Steinberg explained, it is our ability to function as kinsman, congregant, citizen, and human being that serves to advance God's design. Bar Yochai, our greatest Jewish mystic, did not remain in the cave. Not even Moses himself stayed on top of the mountain too long; even he was ordered to return to his people to live in the company of the everyday world. Our spiritual heroes always bring the extraordinary back into the ordinary, the sacred to the mundane, or, as the prayer book says over and over, carry the hope that the peace of the heavens is brought upon us, Israel and humanity.

From Elijah in the cave, to Jesus in the desert, to Mohammad's night journey, this is the oldest story of all – the call to enter another world in order to acquire wisdom and experience not available in the here and now. Each one of us, I suppose, if we chose to do so, could linger in the wild rumpus of those alternative realities, and perhaps someone would even suggest that we be made king of Where the Wild Things Are. But as Jews, more appealing than being crowned the philosopher king of the wild things, is our hope to return to the place where we are loved – to bring that other world back into this one, always returning home, hopefully in time to find our supper still hot. It is the oldest story of all, but the Jewish version always ends here – in this world, with our family, our fellow citizens, and our obligations – each and every day, tending and tilling the very fields of this earth that God has given us all.

(Delivered the week of the passing of Maurice Sendak.)

"Liberty and Its Limits"

From the Garden of Eden onward, humanity has been confronted with the delicate balance of personal freedom and its limitations. "Be fruitful and multiply, fill the earth and master it." (Gen 1:28) Our very first command is a libertarian's dream, as Jefferson noted, "The God who gave us life, gave us liberty at the same time." To be human, it would seem, meant to be free. And then on the heels of that first command came the second one, "Of every fruit of the Garden you are free to eat, but as for the tree of knowledge, you must not eat of it ..." (Gen 2:15) Not one chapter has elapsed and the limitless liberty endowed to us by our Creator is limited. First, what we can eat; then how long we will live, what we can know and what we may do. It is this state of affairs – this tension between personal liberty and its limitations – that has been our lot, as individuals and as a society, ever since. We seek, we hope for, we aspire toward, and believe in that Edenic state of unbridled personal liberty, but we know that for us to exist as a functioning society, that liberty must come with limitations.

Think about any issue in the news today. It is this tension that sits at the core of so many of them. As Americans we hold no right more sacred than our ability to be free to speak our mind freely, a core value codified in the First Amendment. This freedom, however, is not absolute, and it is in the balancing act between this freedom and its exceptions, certainly in this election cycle, that the First Amendment remains one of the most controversial and contentious components of American jurisprudence. Or, if you like, consider free markets. Four years into serving this community I am just starting to understand the business section of the paper, but from what I can make out, an incredible amount of time, energy, and political capital is being spent right now on determining just how free our markets should be. Economic liberty is also a core value, part of our self-definition as a nation, and yet we know that there are profound consequences to a system left to its own devices. Or, if you like, consider questions regarding sexuality. Whatever your views may be, all the recent posturing on sexual preference ultimately comes down to a question of personal liberty and its limitations. If one truly believes that the consenting acts of two adults are nobody's business but their own, then who is the government to use its coercive power to interfere with those freedoms? Nevertheless, it is a sign of moral responsibility, not prudishness, to ask whether, if ever, the public interest should extend its reach into our private affairs.

At the crux of all these debates – political, economic, sexual, and others – lies the question of liberty. It is one of our inalienable rights and we bristle at the suggestion that it be limited. And yet, no matter what the sphere at hand, we know from experience and reason that liberty without limits is nonsensical and dangerous.

The late, great Sir Isaiah Berlin, one of the dominant philosophers of his generation, made a famous distinction between two conceptions of liberty: negative and positive. Negative liberty refers to freedom from any constraints or coercion. The person who is, as the song goes, "free to be you and me" is the person who suffers no interference from any external force that would compromise that person's ability to do or be all that she or he seeks to be. Positive liberty, on the other hand, is not about external impediments to liberty, but internal ones – about an individual's ability to control his or her own destiny and achieve self-mastery. The person who cannot help but go to the cupboard for a late night snack, for instance, does not suffer from any negative liberty; the Double Stuff are readily and freely available. That individual, however, in the inability to control his or her own cravings, is in the second sense not free, fettered by the internal passions standing in the way of self-realization, or in this case, self-discipline. And, as Berlin explains, the challenge we face is how to ensure that one liberty is not bought at the price of another. How do we make sure that our own access to free speech, education, healthcare, or other privileges does not impede another's right to the same.

The Jewish discussion on the nature of liberty begins not with Berlin, but with the Bible, specifically this week's commandment to "Proclaim liberty throughout all the land unto all the inhabitants thereof." (Leviticus 25:10) More important than the verse on the Liberty Bell in Philadelphia is the context in which *dror*, liberty, would be proclaimed. For seven cycles of seven years the land is to be sown, and in the fiftieth, the Jubilee year, everything shall return to its initial holding. Slaves are redeemed, land is returned, and debts are released. Whatever the strengths and weaknesses of such an arrangement may be, the ethic it embodies is clear enough. Our resources, our land, our 'selves' are in truth not ours – everything ultimately belongs to and serves God. The paradox of the biblical Jubilee is that one and the same act both proclaims our liberty and asserts our obligations to God and the community. If anything, the Jubilee proclamation of freedom affirms that not only are liberty and collective obligation not opposites of each other, but they are necessarily interdependent for a just society to exist.

It would be easy enough to understand, and many have, a life of liberty and a life of obligation to be mutually exclusive. For Jews this conversation is not new. Indeed, as long as there have been Jews living by the *mitzvot*, there have been those who have contended that it is these very commandments that limit the full expression of our humanity. Did God, the thinking goes, really create us in the Divine image only to then place restrictions on how we can express that humanity? And yet, if the Biblical concept of Jubilee is any indication, given the choice of being either totally free or totally obligated, as Jews we reject the choice as a false one. Rather it is in the service of God and in the performance of *mitzvot* that we express our freedom. The iconoclast Israeli intellectual Yeshayahu Leibowitz (interestingly, a childhood contemporary of Berlin's in Riga, then part of Russia), forcefully argued that the whole purpose of *mitzvot* is to demonstrate that we are capable of transcending our base human selves. By limiting what we eat, by limiting the days we work, by limiting with whom we sleep, we are giving expression to something akin to Berlin's positive freedom, in that we are proclaiming liberty by demonstrating our ability to transcend our physiological impulses. Only in expressing our limitations is humanity liberated from the chains of biology; only in accepting the yoke of

Torah is the yoke of nature lifted. And in the case of the biblical Jubilee, only one who is free can declare service to God, and only one who lives in service to God can be free. Tellingly, the rabbis explain that the word to describe God's inscription on the tablets of the law – *harut* – may also be read *herut*, meaning freedom. As the rabbis continued, "The only free person is one who is concerned with Torah." (*Avot* 6:2)

While there exists no shortage of biblical precedent and varied philosophic defenses, we need only examine the particulars of our own lives to recognize that a life of freedom and a life of obligation are two sides of the same coin. Think of a person you love, a job you love, anything in this world you love. Our loves, our passions are inevitably found in those spheres that permit us to express the fullness of our selves within the bounded contours and cadences of existence. Like a poet maintaining verse, a musician holding a rhythm, a painter following technique, or one lover covenanted to another, we find the artistry of our lives in the dynamic interplay of form and freedom. Somewhat counter-intuitively, it is in the very relationships in which one allows oneself to exist fully in categories that define and delimit identity – 'spouse,' 'parent,' 'citizen,' 'Jew' – that one actually finds the grandest possibility of self-realization.

It seems to me that a strident defense of liberty must go hand in hand with a willingness to consider the limitations necessary to protect that liberty. The defense of free speech or free markets or free anything must never come at the cost of denying others the very things we claim to hold dear. The delicate balance of liberty and obligation in the Jewish sources is instructive because it sees no contradiction between autonomy and obligation on an individual or communal level. It is this lesson that liberty without limits is really just another form of servitude that is a desperately needed correction to our present national discourse.

In just a week, we will be celebrating the festival of Shavuot, the holiday when the Israelites were made a nation at Mount Sinai. As the rabbis tell it, God shopped around the law from nation to nation, offering it to each and every one. Upon hearing that the law would limit their liberty to steal, to murder, to commit adultery, one by one the nations refused God's offer. Only the Israelites accepted the Torah sight unseen. *Na'aseh v'nishma*, "we will do and we will listen." Only the Israelites understood that if they wanted to be a holy nation, they would, of their own volition, have to give a little bit of themselves in the process. And they did, with love and with joy. It was not a concession, it was a moment of growth and transformation, and it was the difference between Israel and every other nation. May each of us, like the Israelites of old, in embracing our obligations embrace our liberty and, in so doing, enable ourselves and each other to achieve the fullness of being that is our right and our blessing.

Naso

"Dialogue between the Generations"

A s I begin my fifth year at Park Avenue Synagogue, I have had many opportunities to reflect on what it means to stand on the cusp of a generational shift in American Jewry. One hundred and thirty years of congregational history, generations of families, the stature of our past rabbis, the stature of our congregants – if there has ever been a synagogue that prides itself on being an institution of American Jewish life, this is the one. And here I am, technically a member of Generation X, born and bred in sunny Southern California no less, part of the MTV generation, more "Star Wars" than "Godfather," more "Thriller" than "Off the Wall," part of the era of Gretzky, Magic, and Bird. Entrusted with the literal and figurative keys to this synagogue, I find that my job comes down to a dialogue between generations, determining how the Judaism treasured by one generation will be received and transmitted by the generation that follows. It is a delicate conversation to manage. On the one hand I need to assure one side that what is most important to them will be passed down unchanged and untarnished. Yet I need the next generation to know that the Judaism I invite them to practice is a response to them and their moment, not that of their parents and grandparents. It is not easy to manage this balancing act, but there is no conversation more important, not only to this synagogue, but to the future of American Jewry.

I was reminded of the sensitivities involved in negotiating this tension last week, when I read an article by my former teacher Professor Jack Wertheimer in the July issue of *Commentary* magazine. Professor

Wertheimer is a historian of the highest rank, past Provost of the Jewish Theological Seminary, a keen observer of the American Jewish scene, a fine human being and a caring Jew. I think I received an A– in his class and I hope my comments this morning won't stop him from being a scholar-in-residence here at Park Avenue Synagogue in the future.

Wertheimer's article is called "The Ten Commandments of American Jewry." I left copies of it in the hallway for you to read once you are home. The article laments the profound and problematic transformations characterizing American Jewry in the last few decades. At our own peril, we have turned our energies towards universal concerns at the expense of being attentive to the Jewish condition. More interested in performing acts of social justice/*tikkun olam*, we neglect tending to our parochial needs. We are more interested in criticizing Israel than in embracing a tribal peoplehood or nationalism. One by one, Wertheimer lists the ten new "commandments" adopted by American Jewry that have superseded the commanding voice of Mount Sinai. In a rush to be pluralistic, non-judgmental, and inclusive, Jewish leadership refuses to draw lines. What's worse, we air our dirty laundry in public, insisting not only that all views be heard, but that these conversations happen in the public sphere – on the web, the *Huffington Post*, and the opinion page of *The New York Times*. So concerned is this rising Jewish generation with celebrating a Jewishness that is personal and meaningful, that the threats Israel faces and the memory of those murdered in the Shoah have been shunted to the background.

Wertheimer doesn't attack me personally, but he does point to a book I edited as representative of what he perceives as the betrayal of Jewish particularism by the next generation. While I am thankful for the free publicity (the book is now available in paperback), what he says about me and my colleagues is not pleasant. He charges that in the next generation's gaze towards our universal condition, we have become blinded to our own needs. In our pursuit of global citizenship, we have abdicated the Jewish claim to the future.

It is a tough pill to swallow, not just for me personally, but in his assessment of the next generation. A bleak picture, a stinging rebuke, and an ominous prophesy for the Jewish future.

Ultimately, there are two questions that really matter. Number one: Is Wertheimer correct in his characterizations? And number two: Is Wertheimer helpful? This morning, I can tell you that as sure as I am that the answer to the first question is "yes, he is correct," I am doubly sure the answer to the second question is a categorical "no, he is not helpful."

Wertheimer is absolutely correct that the pendulum of Jewish life, which fifty years ago swung towards a post-Holocaust, Israel-in-crisis, parochial set of concerns has now swung in the other direction, towards universalism. Many of his characterizations are spot on, in that the present language of Jewish life seeks to be pluralistic, personal, non-judgmental, inclusive, meaningful, willing to be critical of Israel, and willing to criticize Israel publicly. Wertheimer wrote it, I agree with him, and I agree that the essays in the book I edited only serve to drive the point home.

But as to whether Wertheimer is helpful or not – on that, I feel the need to respond. It strikes me that with all his insight, all his finger wagging, all his intergenerational condescension, Wertheimer misses a significant point: a dialogue goes two ways. Nowhere does Wertheimer admit the inconvenient question of how American Jewry got here in the first place. There is no causality in Wertheimer's thinking. Nowhere is there an allowance that the challenges facing present-day Jewry were bequeathed by the very leaders who are now so critical.

I could, if I wanted to, also write an article in *Commentary*. I could write that the present deficiencies in Jewish literacy are a consequence of a decades-long troubled model of congregational education. I could write about the challenges presently facing Jewish day schools, and I could point a finger at the past generation for having failed to create a sustainable and affordable model for my peers and myself who now want to send our kids to Jewish day school and Jewish summer camps.

I could ask publicly why it is that non-Orthodox synagogues have such a hard time getting a community to turn out to pray on a Friday night or Shabbat morning. But in order to ask that question in its fullness, I imagine I would probably have to examine the decisions made by the past generation, who in investing enormous resources in building magnificent houses of worship, somehow forgot that the most important investment in building synagogue life is the cost-free act of taking your children to *shul* and teaching them the value and power of prayer in community.

I share Wertheimer's concern about my generation's slackening connection to the American Jewish Establishment. But who is really to blame? The next generation who isn't affiliating or the past generation for its repeated and continued inability to redefine, re-brand, and re-structure itself? Is it really so difficult to understand why someone would hesitate to support organizations that – in some cases, even by the quiet admission of some of their own leadership – have outlived their initial mission?

I also worry about a perceived distancing of young American Jewry from Israel. Somewhere along the way it has become easier for a Jew to openly criticize Israel than to openly love it. But that conversation didn't start this spring with Peter Beinart; that conversation started forty-five years ago with the building of settlement blocs that, to the best of my knowledge, run contrary to the present Israeli policy of a two-state solution. Are we really ready to label someone anti-Zionist just because they have difficulty comprehending policies that are in-comprehensible to Israelis themselves?

I could, if I wanted to, write an article in *Commentary* about the problem of Jews under forty holding prickly Jewish conversations in the public domain. I could, but I won't, because Jews under forty are not the readership of *Commentary* magazine.

I could, if I wanted, do all these things. I could, but I won't. Why? Because it strikes me as both ungracious and unproductive to lay my present-day problems at the doorstep of another generation. Wertheimer's article is counterproductive because rather than engendering intergenerational discussion it engenders intergenerational hostility. I have neither the time nor the inclination to explain myself to a generation that created the very challenges facing the Jewry that I have been entrusted to educate and inspire and then questions the manner in which I do so.

Intergenerational finger pointing does not serve the Jewish future. We can all play that game, but I choose to work on the assumption that the past generation, like my generation, does what every passionate generation of Jews has done – the very best it can. I would rather just say "thank you." Thank you for everything you did and continue to do. For doing your best, for freeing Soviet Jewry, for AIPAC, for my education, for Jewish Studies Chairs across America, for Israel, for honoring the memory of those murdered in the Shoah. Thank you for Phillip Roth, for Woody Allen; thank you for USY, thank you for JTS, thank you for it all. Whatever the gripes I may have with the Jewish world I received, they are infinitesimal when compared to my full-throated gratitude for the gifts that I can never repay and can only pray that I live up to.

But now it is time to allow for the possibility that the landscape is different than it was in the past generation.

If I choose to build a caring community whose mission is defined as seeking "pride" and "joy" and "meaning" in being Jewish, it is because the calling cards of "Never Again" and "Israel in Crisis," important as they are, have proven to be inadequate drivers for contemporary Jewish identity.

If the Judaism I teach and preach is a Judaism that seeks authenticity without judgment, inclusiveness not guilt, and personal meaning before ideological loyalty, then maybe it is because I think the landscape of Jewish life has changed and past formulations do not stand a chance in the present marketplace of ideas.

If I find myself emphasizing aspects of Jewish identity that speak to universal concerns like *tikkun olam*, maybe it is (a) because as far back as Abraham, God commanded us to be a light unto nations, and (b) because for a non-Orthodox Jewry that does not have a natural point of contact with Jewish observance, is it really such an odd tactic to seek Jewish engagement by way of common ethical concern? After all, when a would-be convert asked the ancient sage Hillel to summarize all of Judaism while the questioner stood on one foot, Hillel responded, "that which is hateful unto you, do not do unto others." For this you need to go to a rabbi, for this you need Judaism?! This is the most universal statement of interpersonal ethics I can imagine. I suspect Hillel knew what many Jewish leaders today know: for the initiate to our faith – the first task is to find an agreeable point of entry and establish common ground. I imagine Hillel's goal, like that of my peers and myself, was to cultivate Jewish communities filled with learned, observant, and passionate Jews. I reject the rhetorical ploy that one must choose between the universal and particular, the cosmopolitan or the tribal. Our model, my model, is based on the belief that by living an engaged Jewish life we are serving not just the Jewish future, but all of humanity at one and same time.

It would be nice, I suppose, to be a rabbi at a time when everyone keeps Shabbat, observes *kashrut*, comes to *shul*, and gives to UJA. Frankly, I don't think such a time ever existed, but if it did, it doesn't exist now. Each one of us is born into the time in which we live and it serves neither us nor any other generation to condescend or blame another. I would like to think that the best thinkers of each generation can find a way to sit down together and have honest and chest-expanding conversations, without condescension, without blame, and discuss how the Judaism we all love so much can find continued vibrancy in an ever-shifting landscape. We all bear the name of the generation that came before us, and we are all invested in the success of the next.

Last night, like every Friday night, I blessed my children at my Shabbat table, the same blessing that we read in this week's *parashah*: "May God bless you and protect you; may God's light shine on you and be gracious unto you; may God's countenance be turned towards you and grant you *shalom*." I draw my children close – *panim-el-panim*, face to face – sharing the Judaism that I have learned and love, holding my breath, nervously aware that my children will confront the world not on my terms, but on their terms, with answers particular to them. I must help shape that future, but ultimately it is not my future – it is theirs. I bless them, smiling inwardly, imagining that day in the not-too-distant future when they too, please God, will hold their breath, blessing their children, my grandchildren, with the words of our tradition handed down for millennia.

B'ha·alot'kha
"My Birthright Experience"

This morning, I want to talk to you about a program called Birthright Israel – a ten-day free trip to Israel for young Jews between the ages eighteen and twenty-six. I just returned from traveling with a Birthright bus that included many participants who grew up at Park Avenue Synagogue, and for which much of the funding came from members of our community.

I have never felt so old in my life! The first night at dinner I sat at a table of twenty-somethings, some of whom I discovered were from my home town of Los Angeles. I overheard that some of them even went to the same high school as I did, and as Jews tend to do in these situations, I initiated a game of Jewish geography. One of the participants perked up and innocently asked if perhaps I had graduated the same year as his father – also a graduate of that high school. It was a dagger through the heart. Imagine how crestfallen I was when I realized that in the eyes of these college students, I was not a big brother and certainly not a peer, but a co-conspirator in that dreaded project known as their parent's generation.

Given my outsider status, I decided to think about what Birthright, called *Taglit* in Israel, is all about. Through the audacious vision and philanthropy of its founders, Birthright – now in its thirteenth, *"Bar Mitzvah"* year – has sent about 300,000 young Jews to Israel … at no cost to them. About 80% come from North America, but Jews from over 50 countries are represented among the approximately 40,000 students who go every year. Significantly, every Birthright bus also includes young Israelis – now numbering about 50,000 – who travel across Israel with the group.

I readily admit that I was initially skeptical of the entire project. Why in the world should the Jewish community prioritize a ten-day boondoggle? In a world of diminishing resources, does it really reflect Jewish values to pay for a party for thousands of kids, many of whom have shown absolutely no sign of Jewish involvement? And why on earth should it be free? For many, but certainly not all of the participants, the $3000 price tag is not an insurmountable barrier of entry. And perhaps most of all, what exactly is the yield on this investment? I love Israel engagement as much as anyone I know, and my passport attests to that fact, but how exactly does sending young adults to Israel serve to bolster the future of Diaspora Jewry?

Before I give you my answer, you should know that others have had the same concerns. Last year, Brandeis University published a longitudinal study of Birthright (http://www.brandeis.edu/cmjs/noteworthy/jewish_futures_taglit.html) meant to research these very questions. Among the results, the study showed that Birthright alumni feel more connected to Israel and more conversant about Israel than non-participants of the same age. Moreover, Birthright alumni attached a higher importance to marrying someone Jewish, raising Jewish children, and building a Jewish home than non-participants.

All this is important, but having just returned from a trip, I think the secret of Birthright is more profound than its influence on marital choice or the ability to speak with confidence about the geopolitics of the Middle East. The power of Birthright is that it unabashedly tells a generation of disaffected Jews, "Come as you are!" The whole point of the trip is that there are no barriers to entry. Rich/poor, tall/short, Ivy League/City College, religious/secular – come as you are, we will take you! And once on the trip you will experience something that you have never experienced in your life – being immersed in a group whose sole shared characteristic is being Jewish. The audacity of Birthright is that it can be understood as as an effort aimed at bending the arc of modern Jewish history. For the last two hundred years or so, the story of the Jewish people has been a tale of Jews desperately trying to balance the competing tensions of being rooted in their particular history and yet fully participating in modern society, members of a unique and chosen people but also part of a shared humanity, citizens of our country all the while connected to a land called

Israel. It is a subject that fills libraries, and it is a balancing act that plays out anecdotally in all our daily lives. We send our kids to secular schools *and* Hebrew Schools, summer camps that aren't Jewish *per se*, but Jewish enough. We ask of our children to experience campus life, engage with a diverse humanity, and think critically about everything, but when you come back home, please do so with a Jew so that you can perpetuate an ancient tradition. I could give a million examples; they all reflect the same condition. To be a modern Jew is a balancing act, and it is a disorienting and exhausting one to say the least.

So when a twenty-something goes on Birthright, consciously or not, she or he experiences something that they have never experienced before: the feeling of being an integrated whole. It is not so different, mind you, than the argument for Jewish camping, except that the bar of entry for Birthright is that much lower. And for a small window of time – ten days to be precise – life makes sense, because being yourself, being Jewish, being proud, connected to the past, and at home in the present can all happen at the same time, without contradiction, without any of the qualifiers or excuses or self-justifying gymnastics of Diaspora life up to that point. The quiet truth about Birthright is that it isn't primarily a trip about hard content or Israel education; it is a trip about Jewish identity. As Maya Angelou once reflected, people may forget what you said or what you did, but people will never forget how you made them feel. Birthright is able to make its participants feel a certain way. I saw these kids compare the *Magen David* necklaces they purchased and wore proudly; I saw them put on *tefillin* on the top of Masada and recite the *Shema* at the *Kotel*. I saw it all and I was deeply moved by their raw and honest and comfortable explorations of Jewish identity. And I would be remiss if I did not also point out the effect on the Israelis who joined their new Diaspora friends. For the first time in their lives, these Israelis had contact (of varying kinds) with a person who is a Jew but not an Israeli. When it comes to the Jewish peoplehood conversation, only Birthright can point to such a track record of putting Jewish people together.

There is more. Birthright is intriguing because unlike so many other programs, it invests not in bricks and mortar but in the most valuable resource we have when it comes to the Jewish future: Jews. It is countercultural because it asks people to support the one thing that a donor cannot put a plaque on: another Jewish soul. And as our tradition teaches, when a single soul is saved, an entire universe is saved. I do believe that when the story of this era of Jewish history is written, there will be three migrations of Jewry that will be discussed: the exodus of Russian Jews from the FSU, the exodus of the Falash Mura from Ethiopia, and Birthright. Each one can be viewed, in all its particulars, as a bold and transformative act of Jewish redemption. In this day and age, when far too many initiatives in the Jewish world feel, as it were, like rearranging the deck chairs, Birthright is one of the very few efforts that has the potential to fundamentally change the playing field.

Why not fully? Why only potentially? Because the truth is that the ultimate test of Birthright does not fall on Birthright but on us – the North American community who receive the Birthright alumni. Thus far, the track record both for Birthright and for the communities on the ground has been, to put it generously, rather checkered. Birthright accomplishes all it can in its ten days, and I am proud of our community's support, but it is really the follow-up that matters. All those kids from Penn and Columbia and SUNY and Georgetown and Bucknell will soon be back on campus, or in their first job, and they will want somewhere to express that yummy feeling they had in Israel. The window of opportunity is open just a crack, and there is a limited chance to open it wide – to act on it, leverage it, build on it – and then it will slam shut and we will all be back to square one.

In short, what is needed is the same sort of philanthropic *chutzpah* and programmatic gumption on the back end of the Birthright investment. A good starting place is that on my bus, for instance, there were talented Hillel professionals from two of the colleges represented, who are now positioned to build on the shared experience and the newly created relationships. But what is really needed is a partnership between Birthright and the communities on the ground whereby a seamless bridge can be established between trip participants and the Jewish professionals and institutions meant to serve and substantiate their Jewish journeys. I have to believe there is some smart person somewhere who can construct a philanthropic algorithm whereby communal funding is offered in a way that forces partnerships between Birthright and local institutions, funding that not only demands results from the local institutions but also serves to perpetuate the sacred work of Birthright. Would it take a lot of *chutzpah*, cooperative spirit, and money? Of course! But not to do so would render the most exciting effort in Jewish renewal stillborn – and that is not something we should be willing to let happen on our watch.

We are not the first Jewish population to seek renewal by way of Israel. The *haftarah* this morning, the prophetic vision of Zechariah, tells of a time like ours that anticipates a return to Zion after exile and a restoration of the Jewish spirit that has been muted for far too long in its Diaspora setting. A joyous vision is proclaimed announcing the key to a Jewish renaissance. "Not by might, nor by power, but by my spirit - declares the Lord of Hosts." (Zechariah 4:6) It is an "aha" moment of the first degree to realize that the ingredients for the Jewish future are embedded right here – in the souls of every Jew waiting to be stirred. A greater "aha" is the realization that that the key to activating a soul, this birthright, is as simple as being in proximity with others similarly longing for self-expression. Zechariah knew it, Birthright knows it. The only remaining question is whether the rest of the Jewish world can position itself to respond to this insight, gently blowing on the embers kindled some thirteen years ago and building a sustained and vital model of Jewish life able to carry us into the Jewish future.

Sh'lah L'kha
"Acting Now For Ever"

Not too long ago, a friend of mine shared with me the difference between a psychotic and a neurotic. A psychotic, he explained, believes that $2+2 = 5$. A neurotic, on the other hand, knows that $2+2 = 4$, but he worries about it all the time.

I kept thinking about his quip last week as I absorbed the newly-published results of the New York Jewish population study. Ostensibly, the data reported in the Jewish and non-Jewish press bodes well for the Jewish future. In the ten years since the last study, there has been a dramatic increase in the New York Jewish population from 1.4 million to 1.6 million Jews, a development which – if you like Jews – is good news. And yet, like the neurotic in the joke, I find myself worrying about the math. Because if you scratch beneath the surface, the narrative behind the numbers is troubling. It seems that there are more Jews for three reasons. First, because Jews, like all Americans, are living longer. So far, so good. Second, because if you define a Jewish household thinly, meaning as a home containing someone who identifies as Jewish, then there are indeed more Jewish homes. But these homes are, at best, Jewish in name only. And third, because the Haredi or ultra-Orthodox community is booming. In other words, it is at the edges – the unaffiliated and disengaged on one end and the ultra-Orthodox on the other end – that the Jewish community is growing. Reform, Conservative, and Modern Orthodox communities – what I will call the engaged middle – are hurting, if not hemorrhaging. We may not sense it here at Park Avenue Synagogue, but I can tell you my colleagues are feeling it. On Thursday evening I attended the Garden Party at the Jewish Theological Seminary and caught up with some of my colleagues from around the New York region. They are terrific Conservative rabbis of historic communities, exemplars of what it is to be a rabbi, not a slouch among them. For each of them, the population study is not news, they have long been living the demographic story it tells. Each one of them sees the trends and is worried for the future of the American Jewish center; each one is worried about the math, as we should be.

This is not the first time we have worried for our future, not the first time we have had to think on our feet. I am reminded of a much darker time, around the year 70 CE, when Jerusalem was besieged by the Romans and Holy Temple sat in ruins. The great sage Rabbi Yochanan ben Zakkai sensed the imminent destruction of the Jewish people, and daringly smuggled himself out of Jerusalem in order to gain an audience with the Roman general Vespasian, who would soon become the Emperor. Granted one request, Ben Zakkai famously replied, "Give me Yavneh and its sages." Ben Zakkai knew he could do nothing before the might of the Romans, but by moving the spiritual center of our people away from the destroyed Temple in Jerusalem to the rabbinic academy of the coastal city of Yavneh, Ben Zakkai reinvented Jewish life in a way that that would sustain the Jewish people to this very day. In acting quickly yet keeping an eye on the big picture, Ben Zakkai modeled a sort of idealistic pragmatism, taking dramatic action in the present in order to ensure a brighter though distant future.

In moments of tumult and transformation, people have a natural tendency to do one of two things, both understandable and both inadvisable. On the one hand, when faced with uncertainty, it is tempting to shift gears completely. Something is not working so we radically redirect our goals, often taking unwise risks and embarking on faddish strategies that ultimately lead to our own undoing. The second tactic is just the opposite. We dig in our heels, turning ostrich-like away from the conditions of the present, resisting the need to change. Fear, inertia, slavish loyalty to the status quo – these are the qualities of many groups that presently sit in the dustbin of history.

In a sense, this is the crux of the Israelites' conundrum in this week's *parashah*. The time is a transitional moment as the Children of Israel prepare to enter the Land. Moses sends out the spies to scout

out the territory ahead. At one and the same time, the Israelites are called on to embrace their long-awaited destiny and to take the bold steps necessary to make that destiny possible. It calls for a new muscle group, because they are asked do two things at once: to reinvent themselves from a people of Exodus to a people of Conquest, all the while understanding that transformation as an expression of the long-established goal of entering the Promised Land of Israel. But the Israelites prove altogether wanting in this challenge. They are so fixated on their present fears and concerns, they lose sight of the future horizon. Neither nimble nor responsive, they miss the window of opportunity, an opportunity that would not be extended again until their children's generation.

The take-home lesson of the failed mission of the scouts is that given the choice of thinking in the long term or thinking in the short term, true wisdom is found in knowing that this choice is not one of either/or but rather one of both/and. Jim Collins, one of the most well-read management gurus of our day, conducted a study of organizations that rose to greatness in their respective domains, consistently outperforming industry indexes. One of the many characteristics that distinguish great companies from others is what he calls a "dual lens" capacity – the ability to zoom out and zoom in rapidly and effectively. Great companies, great organizations, great people are able to "zoom out," understanding the landscape and not wavering from a disciplined commitment to long term goals. But these individuals are also able to "zoom in," responding effectively to changing conditions with empirical creativity. Forward-looking people possess this dual lens, able at one and the same time to steadily see things through, but also be ready to make deliberate course corrections when necessary to arrive at their goals.

While Collins doesn't quote him, I was reminded of one of Ben Zakkai's most famous teachings: "If you have a seedling in your hand, and you hear that the Messiah has come, first plant the tree and then go greet the Messiah." Our faith, while ever aspirational, has always contained a healthy dose of this worldly pragmatism. We pray and hope and dream for things in the chronological or theological future; we never stop thinking about tomorrow, but we know that our moment of impact is today. We plant the seedlings in the here and now, ever mindful of our obligations to the future.

It strikes me as altogether premature to announce the death of liberal Judaism (as some have in the past few days). Deep in my heart, I believe that there exists not just a place, but a desperate need for exactly what this congregation and like-minded congregations are committed to doing: to create a dynamic expression of Jewish life that is both traditional in its orientation and modern in its inclinations. A faith that embraces a commitment to a particular people and land, but also embraces our shared humanity. A Judaism that is responsive to the longings of every searching soul to feel the caress of God's presence, yet shudders at the thought of fundamentalism. These values are not regnant leftovers from a bygone age, but ongoing and uplifting ideals to which we aspire and remain committed. It is not a need for market share that drives my rabbinate. It is the belief that what we are seeking to do here is right, is needed and yes, is the most authentic expression of Judaism our age offers. I would not dedicate my spiritual existence to a compromise position and neither should you. Like the scouts of the Torah reading, the American Jewish center lacks the conviction and passion and fortitude to enter its next stage of existence. Yes, course corrections are in order. Only a fool would dare ignore the warning signs the new data contains. In order to take the next steps, new ideological and programmatic ideas are needed for Conservative Judaism and other movements. I am not yet ready to give it full articulation and as we enter the summer months I am comfortable ending the season with a cliffhanger. But let there be no mistake. While the means may be in need of modification, our long term goals remain the same. Neither rash nor reckless, we zoom in and we zoom out, informed and responsive to the present, all the while committed to the long term vitality of our way of life.

I shared with you a story of one "Ben" – Ben Zakkai, and I will leave you with a story of another famous "Ben" – Ben Gurion, the first prime minister of Israel. It is a story I was reminded of last week when I visited Tel Aviv's Independence Hall – the historic site of the signing of Israel's Declaration of Independence on May 14, 1948. The decision to proclaim independence did not come without heated debate. While the world was well aware well of Britain's anticipated exit from Palestine on May 15, 1948, it was not at all a foregone conclusion, not even within the Zionist leadership of the day, that the time was right to declare a Jewish homeland in Palestine. After all, the thinking went, if a State were to be declared, the attacking Arab armies would render it dead on arrival. And while we now know that President Truman would recognize the State just eleven minutes after its proclamation, two days before, every signal indicated otherwise. Marshall had indicated to Moshe Shertok (who as Moshe Sharett, would become Israel's first Foreign Minister) that no help would be coming from the United States and it was well known that the State Department had no interest in being pulled into a war against the Arabs. Even Zionist leaders in the U.S. hedged – the time was not yet ripe, the pieces not in place for a declaration. As the story goes, it was on May 12, 1948 that David Ben Gurion encountered these mounting internal and external doubts. But he believed that buried somewhere within the fractious debate was an exciting promise of Jewish destiny. It was on that day that he stood up in his quasi-cabinet and famously proclaimed: *Haverim – achshav o l'olam lo*, "Friends, it is now or it is never." This was not an impulsive act. Just the opposite, it was at that moment that some 2000 years of Jewish history converged on a single point in time and Ben Gurion understood that it was time to flick the switch of destiny. And he did. And a new chapter of our people's history was opened. Over the next two days, the declaration was drafted, to be read and signed on Friday afternoon, May 14, at 16 Rothschild Boulevard.

The Judaism we enjoy, the Israel we are grateful for, the blessings of our lives, exist because leaders like Ben Zakkai and Ben Gurion were able to do the exact thing that great leadership has always been asked to do. To zoom out and see the grand arc of history, and zoom in with a courageous and audacious response that will carry our people towards the fulfillment of God's ancient promise. That promise remains before us now as always. May we have the *chutzpah*, the creativity, the discipline, and the stamina to make decisions in the short term ever loyal to our long term ideals and, in so doing, plant the seedlings today that will be enjoyed by the generations to come.

Park Avenue Synagogue

The Park Avenue Synagogue – *Agudat Yesharim*, the Association of the Righteous – was founded in 1882. From modest beginnings, it has grown into the flagship congregation of the Conservative Movement.

In 1882 a group of German-speaking Jews founded a synagogue and named it Temple Gates of Hope. A church building at 115 East 86th Street was converted into a synagogue and soon the new congregation was known as the Eighty-Sixth Street Temple. Some twelve years after its founding, the synagogue joined together with Congregation Agudat Yesharim, which became the Hebrew name of the congregation, and which appears on the cornerstone of the Rita and George M. Shapiro House at the corner of Madison Avenue and 87th Street. In this congregation the sermons were still preached in German. Later amalgamations were to come. A nearby synagogue, the Seventy-Second Street Temple, itself a product of the earlier merger of Beth Israel and Bikkur Cholim, two congregations that had their beginnings on the Lower East Side in the 1840s and moved uptown to Lexington Avenue and 72nd Street in 1920, merged with the Eighty-Sixth Street Temple – Agudat Yesharim.

In 1923 the Eighty-Sixth Street Temple petitioned the State of New York to change its name to Park Avenue Synagogue. A new sanctuary was constructed on 87th Street three years later and dedicated in March 1927. This building remains the present-day sanctuary. In 1928 the last of the mergers took place when Atereth Israel, a congregation of Alsatian Jews who worshiped in their building on East 82nd Street, added their strength to the Park Avenue Synagogue.

Designed by architect Walter Schneider in 1926, the synagogue building is Moorish in architecture and is one of the last synagogues to have been built in this style, which first became popular in the 1850s in Europe. It features one of the most beautiful cast stone façades in New York and a hand-painted *bimah*. Moorish decoration is used throughout the interior of the sanctuary, from Arabesque dadoes to the design for the domed ceiling.

In 1954 a new building was dedicated in memory of Rabbi Milton Steinberg, who had come to the Park Avenue Synagogue in 1933. It was designed by Kelly and Gruzen with architect Robert Greenstein (a Park Avenue Synagogue congregant and former student of Le Corbusier). The renowned American artist Adolph Gottlieb was commissioned to design its stained glass curtain wall façade, the largest continuous expanse of stained glass of its time. Gottlieb's images were intended to reflect Rabbi Steinberg's teachings, which advocated the integration of traditional Jewish practice within modernity and American experience.

In 1980 this building was incorporated into the Rita and George M. Shapiro House, housing the educational facilities of the synagogue. It features a distinctive rusticated façade of Mankato limestone, the color of Jerusalem stone when fully matured, and was designed by Bassuk Panero & Zelnick architects and modified by Schuman, Lichenstein, Calman & Efron with the assistance of James Rush Jarrett and Dean Bernard Spring of the School of Architecture at City University.

Prominently displayed on its façade are two bronze sculptures by Nathan Rapoport, "Tragedy and Triumph." The lower bas relief depicts Dr. Janusz Korczak surrounded by the children of his orphanage in Warsaw as they were deported to their death at Treblinka. The upper panel depicts three Israelis – a pioneer, a soldier, and an older man – carrying back to Israel the Menorah that was removed from the Temple by Titus and the Romans during Jerusalem's destruction. The inscribed dedication reads: "To the sacred memory of the million Jewish children who perished in the Holocaust." Above the dedication is the Hebrew word *Zakhor* – Remember. Dedicated as a living memorial to the Holocaust, this building expresses Park Avenue Synagogue's hope that the memory of these children will inspire new generations of educated and proud Jews and ensure the continuity of Jewish tradition, history, faith, and heritage.